YOUTH BIBLE STUDY GUIDE
Following God

Tavistock Methodist Church

 Presented to

Ben Hannah

29th November 2015

'Your word is a lamp to my feet and a light for my path.' Psalm 119 vs 105

Youth Bible Study Guides

Sexuality

Following God

Image and Self-Esteem

Peer Pressure

Father God

Jesus Christ and the Holy Spirit

Sin, Forgiveness and Eternal Life

Church, Prayer and Worship

Sharing Your Faith

Suffering and Depression

Giving

Hunger, Poverty and Justice

YOUTH BIBLE STUDY GUIDE
Following God

COMPILED AND WRITTEN BY
CHIP AND HELEN KENDALL

Authentic

Copyright © 2009 Chip and Helen Kendall

18 17 16 15 14 13 12   7 6 5 4 3 2 1

First published 2009 by Authentic Media
This revised edition published 2012 by Authentic Media Ltd
Presley Way, Crownhill, Milton Keynes, MK8 0ES.
www.authenticmedia.co.uk

The right of Chip and Helen Kendall to be identified as the Authors of this Work
has been asserted by them in accordance with the
Copyright, Designs and Patents Act 1988.

All rights reserved. No part of this publication may be reproduced, stored in a retrieval system, or transmitted in any form or by any means, electronic, mechanical, photocopying, recording or otherwise, without the prior permission of the
publisher or a licence permitting restricted copying.
In the UK such licences are issued by the Copyright Licensing Agency,
Saffron House, 6–10 Kirby Street, London, EC1N 8TS.

British Library Cataloguing in Publication Data
A catalogue record for this book is available from the British Library

ISBN-13: 978-1-86024-825-2

Scripture quotations are taken from the Authentic Youth Bible, Easy-to-Read Version™
(Anglicized edition) © 2012 Authentic Media Ltd. Used by permission.
All rights reserved.

Extracts taken from:
Josh McDowell, *Youth Devotions 2*, Tyndale House, 2003
Ems Hancock and Ian Henderson, *Sorted?*, Authentic, 2004
Andy Frost and Jo Wells, *Freestyle*, Authentic, 2005
Chip Kendall, *The Mind of Chip K: Enter at Your Own Risk*, Authentic, 2005
Shell Perris, *Something to Shout About*, Authentic, 2006

'Sometimes He Comes in the Clouds' Steven Curtis Chapman
© 1995 Peach Hill Song /Sparrow Song/Adm. by Small Stone Media BV,
The Netherlands. Used by permission

Cover and page design by Temple Design
Cover based on a design by Beth Ellis
Printed in Great Britain by Bell and Bain, Glasgow

Trust the LORD completely,
and don't depend on your own knowledge.
With every step you take, think about what he wants,
and he will help you go the right way.
(Proverbs 3:5,6)

Chip Kendall (formerly of thebandwithnoname) is a singer/songwriter/ communicator who's passionate about modelling something great for this generation. He now spends his time performing live with his amazing band, speaking at events and conferences, leading worship and going into high schools with 'Test of Faith' science weeks to explain the Christian message to teenagers. Chip's first book, *The mind of chipK: Enter at your own risk* has helped loads of young people grow in their faith. Chip is also pioneering a new movement called 'MYvoice' with Cross Rhythms Radio and presents some youth programming for God TV.

www.chipkendall.com

Helen Kendall has spent 10 years working for Innervation Trust as both Team Leader for thebandwithnoname and Assistant Director of the Trust. She now works with their BeBe Vox and Pop Connection projects. Along with writing these study guides Helen has spent time working on the brand new ERV Youth Bible and dancing as part of Manchester-based Allegiance Dance Crew. Helen also makes a mean tray of peanut butter cupcakes which she enjoys eating with Chip and Cole (their son).

Chip and Helen currently live in Stockport, UK.

Thank Yous

First up, thanks to Malcolm Down and all the rest of the team at Authentic for giving us the opportunity to work on these study guides, it's been a blast. To everyone at SFC, who read the books and gave us your thoughts, we appreciate the feedback. Thanks to the lovely Lucy West for the fantastic photos, and Kylie for the typing. To everyone who talked to Chip for the 'people clips', thanks for your honesty and willingness to put up with the quirky questions. A really huge thank you everyone at Audacious City Church for being an amazing church family. Thanks to Brian and Norma Wilson for their 'hidden pearls' of wisdom. We loved your perspective on things. Finally, big thanks to all the authors whose work we have used in this book. You are an inspiration.

CONTENTS

Instructions / 9

Introduction / 11

LIFE LESSON 1 – VOICES AND CHOICES / 13

Cricket / 15

Finding God's will is an attitude issue / 16

God's plan for me / 19

LISTEN! / 23

Give me wisdom / 25

How to listen to God / 27

God's Word / 30

What can I do? / 33

SOMETIMES HE COMES IN THE CLOUDS / 36

Swimming in the river and digging the well / 38

God's will on two levels / 40

REALITY CHECK – DO I LISTEN TO GOD'S VOICE? / 42

LIFE LESSON 2 – THE DARK SIDE / 45

Body slam / 48

Fisticuffs / 52

Spiritual attack / 54

Schizophrenic skin / 57

LIFE LESSON 3 – DISCIPLESHIP AND ACCOUNTABILITY / 61

Living together in peace / 63

What is discipleship? / 64

What is accountability? / 66

God's will, your desires – they fit / 69

PROPHECY / 71

Prophecy today? / 74

Moving in the prophetic / 77

REALITY CHECK – MAKING DISCIPLESHIP WORK FOR *ME* / 79

LIFE LESSON 4 – 'FOLLOW ME' / 81

Whose rules will rule? / 83

Epic tales / 85

'Go!' But why don't we want to? / 86

Commissioned 110 per cent / 88

PRACTICAL HELP / 91

But how? / 94

Getting to know God / 97

Time out / 99

REALITY CHECK – MY PERSONAL STRATEGY / 101

Further recommendations / 103

INSTRUCTIONS

The book you're holding in your hands is a study guide. It's a compilation of lots of other books written about this subject. It might not make you the world's expert on the subject, but it should give you lots of useful information and, even better, it should give you some idea of what the Bible has to say about . . . FOLLOWING GOD.

What is a 'reaction box'?

Throughout the book, you'll find these helpful little reaction boxes. We've added them so that you can decide for yourself what you think about what you've just read. Here's what one should look like once you've filled it in:

Pretty simple really . . .

Circle the face that reflects how you feel about it.

Tick the box that shows what you think about it.

Fill in any thoughts you have about what you've learned on the lines provided.

What are 'people clips'?

Just so you don't get too bored, we've added a bunch of 'people clips' to each study guide. These are people just like you, who were happy for us to pick their brains about various related topics. Who knows? Maybe you'll find someone you recognize.

What are 'hidden pearls'?

Everyone needs some good old-fashioned 'grandparently' advice, so we collected some pearls of wisdom from our friends Brian and Norma Wilson (aged 86 and 85), which you can find scattered throughout the book.

What is a 'reality check'?

Finally, throughout the book you will come across sections called 'Reality check'. These should provide a chance for you to apply what you've been learning to your own life experiences.

Other than that, the only rule that applies when reading this book is that you HAVE FUN! So start reading.

Chip & Helen

Introduction
GOOD ADVICE ON GOOD ADVICE

The world is full of people offering some pretty rubbish advice. You can find them in the playground at school, on daytime TV talk shows, even in newspaper and magazine columns. Ever seen a horoscope? Perfect example. You've got to be kidding me if you think I'm going to believe someone who stares at the stars all day, (apparently) knows all about how my day will turn out simply because of what month I was born in. How lame is that? Probably not the best place to turn for guidance. In fact, *definitely* not the best place to turn to *at all*.

The Bible, on the other hand, is referred to as 'the good book'. That's because it's packed with tons of *good* advice. It even offers good advice on where to find more . . . well . . . good advice. Just check out what this guy wrote in Psalm 23. Pay special attention to what he says about how God leads him. (Hint: it comes around the middle.)

> The LORD is my shepherd.
>   I will always have everything I need.
> He gives me green pastures to lie in.
>   He leads me by calm pools of water.
> He restores my strength.
>   He leads me on right paths
>   to show that he is good.
> Even if I walk through a valley as dark as the grave
>   I will not be afraid of any danger,
>   because you are with me.
> Your rod and staff comfort me.
>
> You prepared a meal for me
>   in front of my enemies.
> You welcomed me as an honoured guest.
>   My cup is full and spilling over.
> Your goodness and mercy will be with me
>   all my life,
> and I will live in the LORD's house a long, long time.

(King David, Psalm 23)

That sounds like some pretty sound advice to me. But what do you think? Have you ever wondered how you can hear God's voice? Do you want to follow his plan for your life? What about all the hurdles that the devil tries to throw in our way? Is there a formula to having a quiet time? If you've asked any of these questions, you are not alone. All throughout time, people have been digging into God's Word like treasure seekers desperate to find gold. What have they been looking for? Good sound advice on all of life's most complex issues.

So let's see what the Bible has to say about . . . **FOLLOWING GOD**.

LIFE LESSON ONE

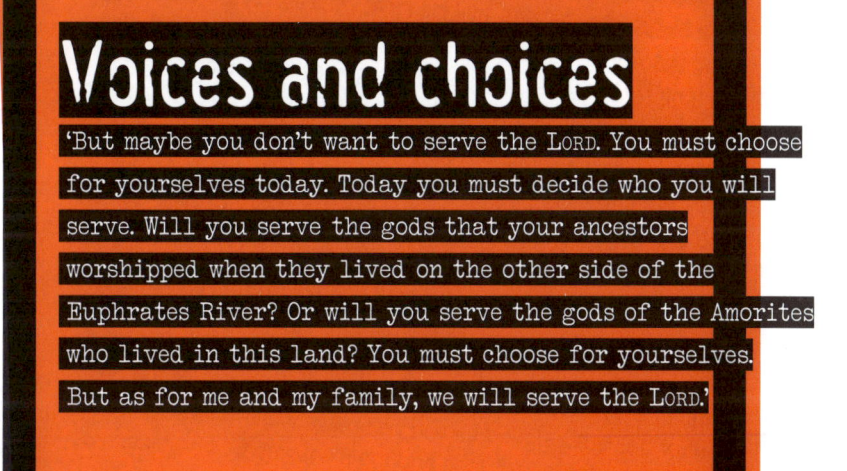

Voices and choices

'But maybe you don't want to serve the LORD. You must choose for yourselves today. Today you must decide who you will serve. Will you serve the gods that your ancestors worshipped when they lived on the other side of the Euphrates River? Or will you serve the gods of the Amorites who lived in this land? You must choose for yourselves. But as for me and my family, we will serve the LORD.'

(Joshua 24:15)

what does the Bible say about FOLLOWING GOD? 13

First up

A very wise woman once told me a story about a young prince whose father, the king, sent him on a very important quest. As the prince set out on his journey, he quickly discovered that as long as he could still clearly hear the instructing voice of his king, he kept making right choices. 'Cross this bridge, avoid that forest, take rest at this particular time...' However, the true tests came once other voices began to distract him, almost completely drowning out the voice of the king. Dragons roaring, trolls laughing, enemies taunting, fair maidens crying for help, even other princes mocking his efforts. In the end, the success of his quest rested entirely on his ability to clearly hear the voice of his father.

It's the same with us, really. Life is full of voices and choices. How do we know which ones we should listen to? God wants us to not only be able to hear his voice all throughout our lives, but he also wants us to choose to follow it. That's how we can get the best out of life. He designed us and he knows what makes us tick. He knows the pitfalls we'll face and the pleasures that wait just around the corner. Decide right now to listen and follow the voice of your Heavenly Father and King.

Pray this prayer (if you agree with it!):

Father in heaven, right now I choose to listen to your voice, follow your plan for my life and obey your instructions. When distractions come, teach me to listen more closely to what you are saying to me and not allow the other voices to drown yours out completely. As I read this book, help me to better understand what the Bible has to say about following you and your precious guidance. In Jesus' name, Amen.

what does the Bible say about FOLLOWING GOD?

Cricket

A **NATIVE AMERICAN AND HIS FRIEND** were down town in New York City near Times Square. It was during the noon hour and the streets were filled with people. Cars were honking their horns, taxicabs were squealing round corners, sirens were wailing, the sounds of the city were almost deafening. Suddenly the Native American said, 'I hear a cricket.' His friend said, 'What? You must be crazy. You can't possibly hear a cricket in all this noise!'

'No, I'm sure of it! I hear a cricket,' the Native American replied. He listened carefully for a moment, walked across the street to a big cement planter where some shrubs were growing. He looked into the bushes, beneath the branches and sure enough he located a small cricket. His friend was utterly amazed.

'That's incredible,' said his friend. 'You must have superhuman hearing!'

'No. My ears are no different from yours; it all depends on what you are listening for.'

'But it can't be!' said his friend. 'I could never hear a cricket in all this noise.'

'Yes it's true,' came the reply. 'It all depends on what is really important to you. Here, let me show you what I mean.'

He reached into his pocket, pulled out a few coins, and discreetly dropped them on the sidewalk. And then, with the noise of the crowded street still blaring in their ears, they noticed every head within 20 feet turn and look to see if the money that tinkled on the pavement was theirs.

'See what I mean? It all depends on what's important to you.'

(Author unknown)

ReactionReactionReactionReaction

CIRCLE:

TICK:
- Total rubbish ☐
- Not sure ☐
- Worth thinking about ☐
- Genius ☐

FILL:
....
....

FINDING GOD'S WILL IS AN ATTITUDE ISSUE

Bible reading: Jeremiah 33:3

'I will tell you important secrets. You have never heard these things before.'
(Jeremiah 33:3)

Pssst . . . here's a hot secret to living a meaningful life. All you have to do is figure out God's will for your life. Then all your worries are over.

Easier said than done, you say? You might know God has a plan for your life, but do you have a clue how to find out what it is?

God *wants* to show you what he wants. But it's easy to get stuck in several wrong attitudes about God's will. Get mired in any of these and you won't escape your confusion about God's will for the important decisions in your life:

GOD'S WILL IS HIDDEN AND I HAVE TO FIND IT. Some students think that discovering God's will is like hunting for Easter eggs. God hides his answers to your questions – and if you can't find them, too bad! That attitude isn't what the Bible shows us about God. He eagerly reveals his will to you if you're willing to receive it.

I DON'T REALLY WANT TO KNOW GOD'S WILL BECAUSE I MIGHT NOT LIKE IT. Some students are afraid God will tell them to marry someone they don't love or spend their lives doing something they don't want to do – like being a missionary in a remote jungle. But is God looking to make you miserable? No. According to Romans 8:32, he wants to graciously give you all things that will fulfil your deepest desires.

I ONLY WANT TO DO PART OF GOD'S WILL. Students with this attitude might never know God's will. It's like trying to drive a car by stepping on the gas and the brake at the same time. One moment you're saying, 'Lord, show me your will,' and the next moment, 'I don't want to do *that* part of your will.' If you don't follow through with what God shows you to do today, why should he show you what to do tomorrow? Commit to do the total will of God.

I WANT TO KNOW GOD'S WILL SO I CAN DECIDE WHETHER OR NOT I WANT TO DO IT. Seeking God's will isn't like shopping for a new car. You can't test-drive his will and then decide if you want to buy it. You either want God's will or you don't. You will never really know God's will until you desire it more that your own.

Put those faulty attitudes side-by-side with the appropriate attitude: **I AM WILLING TO DO GOD'S WILL, WHATEVER IT IS.** The only attitude God will reward is a willingness to accept God's will even before you know it. It's the attitude expressed by the psalmist who wrote, 'My God, I am happy to do whatever you want. I never stop thinking about your teachings' (Psalm 40:8). God is eager to share his plans and counsel with you – if you are eager to obey.

Josh McDowell, *Youth Devotions 2*, **Tyndale House, 2003**

ReactionReactionReactionReaction

CIRCLE:

TICK:

Total rubbish ☐   Not sure ☐   Worth thinking about ☐   Genius ☐

FILL:

....
....
....
....
....

Name: Ben Yip
Age: 15
Town: Orpington
Current status: music student

PEOPLE CLIP

What is your favourite band at the moment?

thebandwithnoname

Have you ever written music before?

I'm working on some tracks

Where do you find inspiration?

Just listening to Tim Hughes talk, really.

How do you feel God speaks to you?

I'm not so sure – I just have a feeling that I have to go and do something.

And you believe that is God?

Yep.

18 what does the Bible say about FOLLOWING GOD?

GOD'S PLAN FOR ME

It's good to know that someone has a plan. But having the plan isn't enough in itself. We want to know that the plan will work. And God has the best qualifications and previous experience to have a plan for your life and for it to work. After all, he made you. Yeah, I know your mum and dad had a part to play (now that's something you don't want to dwell on) but it's a bit like your trainers . . .

Being a designer label

TAKE A LOOK AT YOUR TRAINERS. Chances are they have a designer's label – that's probably why you chose them. Someone at that company designed your trainers, and had a purpose and plan for them (e.g. to be comfortable, fashionable, good for running/skating in etc.) *someone else* in another factory made them. God designed you with a purpose and a plan, your mum and dad, like the worker in the shoe factory, physically put you together, but God was the designer. That's why we can trust his plan – because we've got his designer label.

The love is in the plan

When Jesus was baptized, a voice from heaven said, **'THIS IS MY SON, THE ONE I LOVE. I AM VERY PLEASED WITH HIM.'** Read it for yourself in Matthew 3:17.

God loves to 'big up' the people he loves, you might not have heard a voice from heaven saying how much God loves you, but the Bible says that he thinks you're amazing! Do you know that God loves you – I mean really loves you? Do you know that he longs for you to know him and trust him further? Do you understand that he could never wish you harm, that he cries with you when you feel alone or when things or situations fail around you? Do you know what it means to have his presence with you every moment of every day? Do you know that he knows every beat of your heart and every longing in your soul? Do you know that God loves who you are? He wants simply to remind you today that he made you as you are. Do you know how much he enjoys looking at you and saying 'I made you'? He longs for you to spend the

what does the Bible say about FOLLOWING GOD? 19

rest of your life in closeness with him, showing others by the way you live that he is alive.

How do you feel about that?

Who better to trust to have a plan for your life than someone who loves you *this* much. So we know that God loves us and therefore wants the best for us. But sometimes it's easy to forget that, particularly when we have had a tough time, or when we compare ourselves to other people who seem to have landed on their feet. Don't you think? However, the Bible is very clear that although this may be our perception, nothing could be further from the truth. God's desire is to bless us and give us good things – all the time.

> We know that in everything God works for the good of those who love him. These are the people God chose, because that was his plan. God knew them before he made the world. And he decided that they would be like his Son.

(Romans 8:28,29)

When we live in the knowledge of this truth, and follow what God is saying to us, the Bible says that we have the promise of his blessings over and around us. (Check this out in Deuteronomy 28:1,2.)

Hidden pearls

'It's really important to attend your church regularly. This means you get information. Older people can give you advice, and if you're wise, you'll listen to what's been said by these older people.'

The point of the plan

Firstly let's look at the big picture. That's hard for us isn't it? When we are trying to hear God or coming to him for guidance, normally it's about a specific thing – what exams should I take? Should I go out with this guy? What should I call my hamster? But that's the small picture, the details of our day-to-day, and God is totally into those kind of details but it's important we check out the big picture first, the overall plan.

So let's get back to basics. **THE BIG, BIG PICTURE IS THAT GOD LOVES YOU** and his plan is that you get saved and love him back, giving you the life you were made to have – life to the full. Great!

But have you ever wondered why, when you became a Christian you didn't just get beamed straight to heaven? If the plan was for you to get saved . . . well, mission accomplished, so why are we all still here then?

After all, almost everything we do as Christians will be a million times better and easier in heaven. We will be able to worship and get to know and love God so much more when we are in his presence for eternity, so no more 'can God hear me?' He's right there in front of you. As for having life to the full . . . heaven rocks! No pain, death, sin, doubt or discouragement – that's life to its fullest.

God wants our lives to be full and fulfilled. A lot of people see God as some sort of heavenly killjoy. But we know that he didn't make us just so that he could then spoil our fun. In fact the exact opposite is true. Jesus said in John 10:10, **'I CAME TO GIVE LIFE – LIFE THAT IS MORE THAN YOU CAN IMAGINE NOW.'** This sounds like a good deal to us!

So what does God plan for us specifically? When Jesus first called his disciples he told them that he was going to make them 'fish for people', (Matthew 4:19). That meant that he was going to use them to bring other ordinary people to know God. This is also one of the last things he said to them whilst he was on earth: 'go and make followers of all people in the world' (Matthew 28:19). The point of being a Christian isn't to live life as if on a beautiful yacht, sunbathing in the knowledge that we are saved, but to help with the lifeboats, joining in with God's rescue mission for others. The plan was for us to know Jesus but also to make Jesus known. In fact if you think about it, the only thing we can't do in heaven is tell other people about Jesus, which must be why we don't go there straight away.

Our great commission is that whilst we are alive, we share with others what he has done for us, not out of some dreadful fear or guilt, but because he first loved us and gave himself up for us.

When you fall in love with someone, you can't shut up about it can you? Everyone you know also has to know. It's natural to tell people. There is no effort and it's the first thing you want to say. When you find out something really exciting or cool, you want to share it with your mates don't you? We should be prepared to give a reason to others for the hope we have in us. The first disciples said, ' . . . We must tell people about what we have seen and heard' (Acts 4:20). They were just desperate for people to know.

God has loved you into his plan; now he plans to help you love others into it too. Part of God guiding you will be about helping you to guide others to him. God has all sorts of things ready for us to do for him.

> God has made us what we are. In Christ Jesus, God made us new people so that we would spend our lives doing the good things he had already planned for us to do.

(Ephesians 2:10)

Of course God is interested in your love life but are you interested in this life of love? This is the first step to guidance? If anything you plan gets in the way of you knowing God or making him known then it won't be part of his plan for your life. The small picture must always fit into the big picture.

Ems Hancock and Ian Henderson, *Sorted?*, Authentic, 2004

ReactionReactionReactionReaction

CIRCLE:

🙂 🙁 😐 ‼️ 😟 😮

TICK:

Total rubbish ☐   Not sure ☐   Worth thinking about ☐   Genius ☐

FILL:

....
....
....
....

22 what does the Bible say about FOLLOWING GOD?

Listen!

'My sheep listen to my voice. I know them, and they follow me. I give my sheep eternal life. They will never die. And while they are under my care, no one can take them from me.'

(John 10:27,28)

what does the Bible say about FOLLOWING GOD? 23

First up

Hearing God's voice is something very special. And yet Jesus promises that all Christians everywhere can actually know his voice. Isn't that incredible? The same voice that spoke the whole universe into existence speaks your name right now. Are you listening? He knows you. Do you recognize him?

In a book that is all about following God and his guidance, we'd be insane not to include a section on hearing and knowing the voice of God. Trust us, he doesn't always choose to speak in a real-life audible voice like when your mates ring you on your mobile. And sometimes he speaks to us in a certain way on one day, and a completely different way the next. Even though God is the same – yesterday, today and forever – we've found that as you go deeper in your relationship with him, your ability to hear and know his voice becomes stronger too.

It makes sense, really. Think about the way you talk to a little baby . . .

'Well hello there little smooshy-mooshy-wooshy. Can you say "poo poo"?'

Then imagine using the same voice to speak to an adult!

'What's that, little guy? You want a promotion at work? Can you say "lah-lah-lah"?'

It simply wouldn't have the same effect, would it? In the same way, God chooses to speak to us in different ways throughout the various seasons of maturity in our lives. But the important thing is that he definitely does speak to us. We've just got to learn how to listen up.

24 what does the Bible say about FOLLOWING GOD?

Give me WISDOM

> Always remember what is written in that Book of the Law. Speak about that book and study it day and night. Then you can be sure to obey what is written there. If you do this, you will be wise and successful in everything you do.

(Joshua 1:8)

Joshua was not in a good place. He had been second to Moses for forty years. He had seen God do amazing things through Moses for this people. He was at the parting of the Red Sea, and witnessed God save Israel. He had accompanied Moses up Mount Sinai and saw the glory of God descend like a cloud. He was present when God gave Moses the law and the covenant. At every landmark of the Exodus, Joshua was there – watching at the sidelines.

And now it was his turn. He must have been bricking it! As Joshua saw it, Moses was God's guy, not him. **HOW COULD JOSHUA BE EXPECTED TO FOLLOW SUCH AN AMAZING LEADER?** God is careful to make sure that Joshua knows the score. The opening chapter of Joshua is all about what God, not Joshua, is going to do. The only direct action God commands Joshua to do is to study his Word. That's the key! Knowledge of the Word will lead to wisdom and success. It's a principle we forget all too easily these days.

> Brothers and sisters, don't think like children... in your thinking you should be like full-grown adults.

(1 Corinthians 14:20)

When I first became a Christian, I dragged up a distant memory from Sunday school that said one of God's favourite prayers in the Bible is that of Solomon and his plea for wisdom. God was so impressed with his humility that he granted him not only wisdom but wealth and honour as well. (Check it out in 1 Kings 3:5–15.) So I thought to myself that maybe it would be a good thing for me to pray for wisdom, too.

So, every day, I would pray, 'God, give me the gift of wisdom. Give me knowledge of you and your heart so I might share it with others.' Now these sorts of prayers never get answered by waking up the next morning and discovering you are the Christian version of the Dalai Lama, but gradually you notice that you know what to say in a difficult situation. You hear God's voice, and can speak advice to someone. There is wisdom in your character that wasn't there before.

what does the Bible say about FOLLOWING GOD? 25

The thing about praying for wisdom is that you don't simply acquire it – it is imparted to you. Wisdom isn't something you simply get, but something passed on. Every day I prayed for wisdom I read and remembered the Bible. Instead of attending church and forgetting everything that had happened the moment I left, the sermons remained with me. I could quote Bible verses that I had only heard once before to people. And the sermons and the readings would always be perfectly timed for when I would need to use them. God was imparting his wisdom to me as and when I needed it. All of it came from the Bible. If you want to influence others around you, if you want God's Word to benefit your surroundings, **LEARN HIS WORD.** The Bible contains God's wisdom. Wisdom is a gift God wants to give us; seek it, God will not deny his children a good thing (Psalm 84:11).

God takes us all on a journey, constantly leading us closer to him. Every day he reveals more of himself to us, more of his heart, his will for our lives. He gives us the gifts that we need and that we seek. The Bible is our means to that revelation. He might use other people, creation, silence or his voice to speak to us, but the permanent source of God's revelation comes through his Word.

Andy Frost and Jo Wells, *Freestyle,* **Authentic, 2005**

ReactionReactionReactionReaction

CIRCLE:

TICK:

Total rubbish ☐   Not sure ☐   Worth thinking about ☐   Genius ☐

FILL:

....
....
....
....

HOW TO LISTEN TO GOD

Tuning into the plan

It's never easy for a boy when he meets his girlfriend's dad for the first time. You are desperate to impress and just hope you won't say anything stupid. I went out with a girl whose dad always sat in front of the telly and never ever talked to me. It was awful. I would try to make conversation about football, cricket, Armenian goat wrestling (I told you I was desperate) and he never answered back or said a word, he would just grunt at me. – Ian

There are times when it can feel like you're praying to a grumpy, grunting God sat in front of the telly, which might be why you are reading this chapter in the first place. But God loves telling us what he thinks, feels and wants to do. In the Bible he used mighty 'in yer face' angels and, believe it or not, a donkey (check out Numbers 22) to get his point across! He used dreams, the weather and a man lying naked on the floor for a few months! Ultimately, he used Jesus, God's Word in flesh and blood.

> The Word became a man and lived among us. We saw his divine greatness – the greatness that belongs to the only Son of the Father. The Word was full of grace and truth.

(John 1:14)

Jesus said we would recognize his voice and **GOD WANTS TO SPEAK TO US**, so why do we struggle so much to hear him, to tune in? Hearing God's voice should be part of the normal experience of being a Christian and yet we can get ourselves tied up in knots about it. There are huge amounts of Christian books dedicated to the subject because it is one thing that is absolutely vital to our belief – and the one thing most Christians find it hard to do consistently.

There have been times when I have heard God speak to me really clearly (to the point of hearing a voice in my head). At other times I have asked and asked and not really seemed to hear anything. I find hearing God **consistently** is my biggest problem. Maybe this is because I am so inconsistent. God hasn't changed. He hasn't stopped speaking, but I may well not be in a good place to hear. Recently, a child in a class I was teaching said he had something to tell me. I was really cross with the children because they were noisy and not getting on with their work. Later in the day, I remembered that I hadn't heard what 'Matthew' wanted to say. Wearily, I asked him to tell me. He said, 'I just wanted to say that I love you, and you are my bestest teacher even when you are cross with us.' If I had heard that earlier on in the day, I would have felt very much better. But I was not in a good place to hear and listen. So I missed out. – Ems

The truth is that we have a God who longs to reveal *himself* to us as well as his *will* for us. There is a person behind the words. It's really important that we remember that when we pray. We are not putting data into some huge cosmic computer and getting a randomly generated answer. We are praying to a person. Hebrews 11:6 says, 'Whoever comes to God must believe that he is real and that he rewards those who sincerely try to find him.'

Believing that God is real and that he wants us to know him personally is the first step to tuning into him. The second is to ask God to help us!

'Do any of you need wisdom? Ask God for it' (James 1:5).

The Bible tells us that as God's children, we can hear what God says. John 10:3 tells us that as God's sheep, we are able to listen to the voice of the Shepherd, Jesus. When we ask God about something, he will answer. (But whether we hear it or not is another matter altogether!)

Ems Hancock and Ian Henderson, *Sorted?,* **Authentic, 2004**

ReactionReactionReactionReaction

CIRCLE:

TICK: Total rubbish ☐ Not sure ☐ Worth thinking about ☐ Genius ☐

FILL:
....
....

PEOPLE CLIP

Name: **Hannah**

Age: **16**

Town: **Bracknell (near Ascot)**

How has God spoken to you recently?

After a seminar I was at recently, a lady came up to me and told me that I had a 'sparkle'. While we were talking, we realized that she had a lot in common with my mum and me. The same name, the same job and some other personal issues. We had a really good chat, and then something amazing happened. I had just given a certain amount of money in the offering, and this lady told me that she had a specific amount of money to give to me. I told her I didn't want it, but she insisted that God had told her to give it to me. Well, it turned out to be the same amount that I'd just put in the offering!

So what are you going to do with the money now?

Put it into a different offering . . .

what does the Bible say about FOLLOWING GOD? 29

GOD'S WORD

chipK's mind

My friend Zulu is incredible. He's like a walking, talking, living, breathing Bible. Seriously, I've never known anyone who can quote so much of the Scripture all the time as part of his daily life. Get this, **HE'S EVEN RECORDED HIMSELF RAPPING THE BOOK OF REVELATION,** and plans on seeing the other sixty-five books of the Bible recorded by other rappers as well!

Zulu is seriously passionate about God's Word. And why shouldn't he be? The Bible continues to be the best-selling book of all time. It was inspired by God's Spirit thousands of years ago and, even still, no one can add to its profound truth. King Solomon, the wisest man who ever lived, wrote a few of its chapters, telling us to search the Bible as if we were digging for hidden treasure. And it's not just because it's a good book. Remember how the 'precious' ring from *The Lord of the Rings* trilogy would grow and shrink to fit the finger of the wearer? Well, in the same way, the Word of God is alive and active, revealing different things to different people at just the right time. On top of that, it's compared to being like the sharpest sword ever, full of power to cut deep into our secret thoughts and desires, exposing us for what we really are. No matter what difficult situation you're experiencing, no matter how many times you've done it before, you can always turn to the Bible for the best advice around.

NOW PLEASE EXCUSE ME WHILE I GO BUST SOME RHYMES FROM LEVITICUS.

God's mind

Your word is like a lamp that guides my steps, a light that shows the path I should take.
(Psalm 119:105)

God's word is alive and working. It is sharper than the sharpest sword, and cuts all the way into us. It cuts deep to the place where the soul and the spirit are joined. God's word cuts to the centre of our joints and our bones. It judges the thoughts and feelings in our hearts.
(Hebrews 4:12)

Ask for good judgement. Cry out for understanding. Look for wisdom like silver. Search for it like hidden treasure.
(Proverbs 2:3,4)

I study your teachings very carefully so that I will not sin against you. LORD, you are worthy of praise! Teach me your laws. I will repeat the laws we have heard from you. I enjoy following your rules as much as others enjoy great riches. I will study your instructions. I will give thought to your way of life. I enjoy your laws. I will not forget your word. Be good to me, your servant, so that I may live to obey your word. Open my eyes so that I can see all the wonderful things in your teachings. I feel like a stranger visiting here on earth. I need to know your commands. Don't keep them hidden from me.
(Psalm 119:11–19)

All Scripture is given by God. And all Scripture is useful for teaching and for showing people what is wrong in their lives. It is useful for correcting faults and teaching the right way to live. Using the Scriptures, those who serve God will be prepared and will have everything they need to do every good work.
(2 Timothy 3:16,17)

Your mind

- **Who wrote the Bible?**
- **What is my favourite Scripture?**
- **Why is it so important not only to read the Bible, but to memorize it?**
- **How often *can* I read the Bible?**
- **How often *do* I read the Bible?**
- **How often *will* I read the Bible from now on?**

Chip Kendall, *The Mind Of ChipK: Enter At Your Own Risk*, Authentic, 2005

Reaction Reaction Reaction Reaction

CIRCLE:

☺ ☹ 😐 😯 😕 😮

TICK:

Total rubbish ☐   Not sure ☐   Worth thinking about ☐   Genius ☐

FILL:

....
....
....
....
....

Hidden pearls

'I must admit that when I was younger, I probably didn't read it [the Bible] as much as I should have done. I always had an excuse and thought I'd do it later. Now we have much more time to read and we realize how important it is and how it would have helped us when we were younger.'

32 what does the Bible say about FOLLOWING GOD?

Listening heart

Maybe one of your teachers or someone in your family has said to you, 'You can't listen and talk at the same time!' We all have two ears and one mouth. So the ratio of speaking to listening should reflect that.

A big part of listening to God is about being quiet. Here are some things you can do to help:

Shut in! Try going to a room where there is no TV, music or any other distractions – if you've got a busy house it might even be the loo, just don't stay there too long!

Shut up! Once you are in a quiet place you need to *be* quiet. Try not to say anything. Try to stop thinking about your problems, the person you fancy or the conversation you've just had. Ask God to help you. If you find your mind wanders that's OK, it happens to all of us. It might help to write down what you keep thinking of, so that you can forget about it until later. But sometimes it's just about telling yourself not to think of it!

Open up! Then ask God to speak to you. Remember, you might not 'hear' a voice but you might 'sense' something. As you practise listening to God, that 'sense' can become familiar. You might remember something you've read in the Bible or heard someone say, or have an idea or picture. This doesn't mean that every time you feel or think of something it's a direct heavenly txt from God but sometimes it might be.

Write it! It's good to make a note of the stuff you feel God has told you.

Discerning heart

Because it's so easy for us to get it wrong, it's important that when we're listening to God, we check it out against the Bible. All of it can be trusted as something God has already said. Therefore, if your heavenly txt doesn't match what God has already said in your Bible's text, then forget it. For example, no matter how cool they try to make it look in the movies, **GOD'S NEVER GOING TO TELL YOU TO ROB A BANK**, even with gadgets and getaway cars. The Bible tells us not to steal. (Dumb example, but you know what we mean!) He doesn't change his mind. Sometimes mobile phone companies go

what does the Bible say about FOLLOWING GOD? 33

a bit weird and the computers break down and you'll get the same txt 3 or 4 times. It keeps coming back, a bit like a boomerang! Another way of knowing (discerning) if you've heard from God is if your heavenly txt keeps coming back. Maybe you read a verse that speaks to you and then go to church or youth group and they are preaching from the same verse and then a mate sends you an email with the same verse at the bottom. You get the idea – if your heavenly txt becomes a boomerang txt then you can be a lot more certain that God is saying something.

Praying with others and consulting those who are wiser and older than us is a great way to test what we have heard (see 1 Thessalonians 5:21). We can also pray for God to bless us with discernment (see Psalm 119:125). It is a very useful thing to possess and makes others feel safe to share things with us. So if you aren't sure about something, ask God for more wisdom on the matter and chat it through with people you trust.

How does God speak?

There are many ways that God spoke to people in the Bible and many ways he speaks today.

Here are some of the ways that God spoke in the Bible:

- Pictures and dreams (e.g. Daniel and Joseph)
- Physical signs (e.g. God was a pillar of cloud by day and fire by night for the Israelites in the desert, see Exodus 13:21)
- Visions and prophecies (e.g. John writing in Revelation; see also Isaiah)
- Poetry and song (e.g. Psalms and Ecclesiastes)
- Prayers (e.g. Hannah in 1 Samuel 2)
- Stories (e.g. parables in the New Testament)
- Actions (e.g. the temple curtain being torn in two when Jesus died, see Mark 15:38)
- Miracles (e.g. Jesus' healings)
- Heavenly messengers (e.g. angel rolling away the stone at the resurrection, see Matthew 28:2)
- Weather (e.g. the calming of the storm, see Luke 8:24)

In the New Testament God no longer spoke just through prophets. God was now speaking through Jesus (see Hebrews 1:1,2) and Jesus gave us the Holy Spirit. He is part of God and loves to be our comforter, helper and challenger, to speak to us and guide us (see John 14:26). As Christians we all have access to the Holy Spirit as he lives within us. He is at work in every Christian and helps us to hear God's voice (see John 10:3).

Ems Hancock and Ian Henderson, *Sorted?*, **Authentic, 2004**

ReactionReactionReactionReaction

CIRCLE:

TICK:

Total rubbish ☐   Not sure ☐   Worth thinking about ☐   Genius ☐

FILL:

....
....
....
....
....
....
....
....
....
....

Sometimes he comes in the clouds

So we always have confidence. We know that while we live in this body, we are away from the Lord. We live by what we believe will happen, not by what we can see. So I say that we have confidence. And we really want to be away from this body and be at home with the Lord. Our only goal is to always please the Lord, whether we are living here in this body or there with him.

(2 Corinthians 5:6–9)

First up

So maybe you're reading all this and you're thinking, 'I've tried so many times to hear God's voice, but sometimes I feel like my prayers are just bouncing back at me off the ceiling!' You are not alone. All Christians feel like this sooner or later. No matter how intently we search for the answer to some specific question or need that we have, it feels as though God just responds with silence.

In times like these I always remind myself of a song by Steven Curtis Chapman called 'Sometimes He Comes in the Clouds'. The chorus and bridge say this:

Sometimes He comes in the clouds
Sometimes His face cannot be found
Sometimes the sky is dark and grey
Some things can only be known
Sometimes our faith can only grow when we can't see
So sometimes He comes in the clouds
Sometimes He comes in the rain
And we question the pain
And wonder why God can seem so far away
But time will show us
He was right there with us

'Sometimes He Comes in the Clouds' Steven Curtis Chapman © 1995 Peach Hill Songs / Sparrow Song / Adm. by Small Stone Media BV, The Netherlands.

When God responds with silence, he may just be growing our faith in him. So don't give up! Keep asking your questions. Keep knocking on heaven's door. The answer could be just around the corner.

what does the Bible say about FOLLOWING GOD? 37

Swimming in the river and digging the Well

There are times in life when you may get those awesome collective experiences. You're at a massive conference listening to a great worship band. The speaker goes through God's Word, and you encounter God and hear him in a way you never do back at home. These are the streams of God's living water. You get refreshed and encouraged – it's all handed to you on a plate. The thing is, it's really easy living waiting for the next opportunity for the stream to flow past you again. I call this being a weekend conference junkie. You have the crash about 3 weeks after you get home, 'cos the world has infiltrated the Christian bubble that was created while you were away. So, depressed that you can't cope any more, all your heart wants to do is return to where it was safe, where it was easy and everything made sense. The trouble is that as good as the experience was, God wants us to go deeper with him. The streams are great but they are short-lived. Sometimes God asks us to dig wells. Digging is hard work, often seeming thankless. You just end up repetitively shifting dirt. **BUT ONCE THE WELL IS FINISHED YOU HAVE A PERMANENT SOURCE OF GOD'S WATER IN YOUR LIFE**. It takes discipline and dedication. It would be so much easier just to hang about waiting for someone else to tell you what to think and what you need to know but Peter commands us to do it ourselves. Be like adults. As my mate realized having not read the fire blanket instructions, life will side-swipe you when you are least expecting it. Wisdom and preparation are the keys to successful living. Life in Christ is about work. Working to keep on track.

Andy Frost and Jo Wells, *Freestyle*, **Authentic, 2005**

ReactionReactionReactionReaction

CIRCLE:

🙂 ☹️ 😐 ‼️ 🙂 😮

TICK:

Total rubbish ☐   Not sure ☐   Worth thinking about ☐   Genius ☐

FILL:

....
....
....
....
....

Hidden pearls

'If I need to make a decision and God seems to be silent on the subject, I'm not averse to asking some older Christian person who I trust, to get advice. Someone further on in the Lord than I am. Sometimes it is difficult when you don't get an answer, you wonder what to do.'

what does the Bible say about FOLLOWING GOD? 39

God's will on two levels

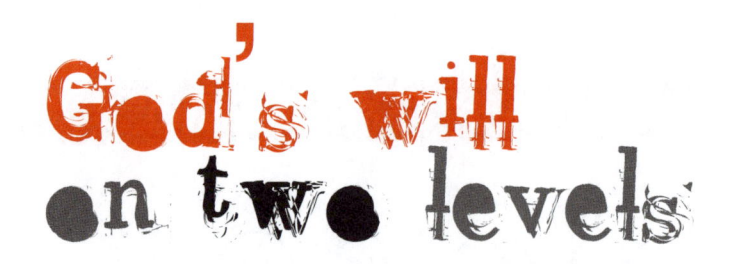

Bible reading: Proverbs 3:1–6

> With every step you take, think about what he wants, and he will help you go the right way.
>
> (Proverbs 3:6)

Carlos walks into his pastor's office feeling a little nervous. But Pastor Keene tries to put him at ease. 'Welcome, Carlos, I'm glad you came. Please sit down. How can I help you?'

Carlos gets right to the point. 'I'm confused about where God wants me to go to college. How am I supposed to find out what he wants me to do?'

'Well, let me start by asking you a few questions,' the pastor begins. 'Have you trusted Christ as your Saviour?'

'Yes sir, 4 years ago at church summer camp.'

'Good. Are you obeying your parents?'

'Well, er, yeah – most of the time, Pastor,' Carlos says, 'but that isn't what I came here to talk about. I want to find God's will for my education.'

'I understand, Carlos,' the pastor says patiently, 'but I want to know if you're already following God's will. If you're not committed to obeying God's will in the obvious, right-here-right-now decisions of life, there's no point looking for what he wants about college.'

When you want to find God's will for your life, you have to look for it at two distinct levels. The first is God's will for all people – what some people call God's *universal* will. The second is God's will for each individual – his *specific* will. Here's the problem: a lot of people try to know God's specific will for their individual lives, all the while ignoring God's universal will.

God's universal will is the clear, unmistakable will for all people you find in the Bible. You know from Scripture, for example, that God's will is for everyone to trust Christ for salvation. Or think about 1 Thessalonians 5:17, which says **'NEVER STOP PRAYING.'** You can be sure it's God's will that everyone grows in a consistent attitude of prayer and closeness with him. God makes other pieces of his universal will equally clear – like loving God and people, obeying parents, sharing your faith with others, remaining sexually pure, etc. You will have a hard time finding God's specific will about things like marriage, college, and career if you waffle on obeying God's universal will.

That doesn't mean you have to be perfectly obedient before God will show you his specific will. Nobody is. But when you set your heart on obeying God's will for everybody in Scripture, you are in the right place to find God's will for your own future.

Josh McDowell, *Youth Devotions 2*, **Tyndale House, 2003**

ReactionReactionReactionReaction

CIRCLE:

☺ ☹ 😐 ❗ 😕 😮

TICK:

Total rubbish ☐   Not sure ☐   Worth thinking about ☐   Genius ☐

FILL:

....
....
....
....

what does the Bible say about FOLLOWING GOD?

Reality Check

DO I LISTEN TO GOD'S VOICE?

Choose the answer that best describes you:

When was the last time I read my Bible?
- a within the past week
- b within the past month
- c I don't even own a Bible

Which of the following best describes my prayer life?
- a me talking to God, and giving him time to answer
- b just me talking to God
- c I only pray when I need God to get me out of an emergency

How do I make big life decisions?
- a through prayer and reading God's advice in the Bible
- b think about it on my own
- c just do what all my friends are doing

When God speaks to me, it usually
- a confirms what the Bible says
- b cannot be found in the Bible
- c contradicts what the Bible says

On a day when I'm really busy, I'll

a depend on God even more by quietly praying throughout the day
b leave praying to the end of the day and then hope that I did alright
c forget about prayer! No time for that

On a day that I'm really lazy, I'll

a prioritize hanging out with God and listening to him
b spend time with friends, then try to include God if I get the chance
c just veg in front of the television all day

ANALYSIS

Mostly answered 'a'

If your answers are mostly 'a's, then it's pretty safe to say that you definitely listen to God's voice, or at least spend a good deal of time trying to. Keep pressing into God and remember that his sheep know (and recognize) his voice.

Mostly answered 'b'

Reading this book should prove to be very helpful for you. You probably want to know God more, but can't seem to figure out what the next step is. Learn to apply what you read in the Bible by practising some of the advice in this book.

Mostly answered 'c'

You need to be challenged to spend more time with God. Listening to his voice is an absolute necessity for getting the most out of life. Get stuck into praying and reading the Bible. This book can be a real turning point for you if you let it. You'll not be disappointed. Promise!

> Don't change yourselves to be like the people of this world, but let God change you inside with a new way of thinking. Then you will be able to understand and accept what God wants for you. You will be able to know what is good and pleasing to him and what is perfect.
>
> (Romans 12:2)

Do you want to know what God's will for your life is? Do you want to know how to do everything that is good and pleasing to him? Well here's how to find the answer: let God change the way you think!

LIFE LESSON TWO

The dark side

Then the devil led Jesus to the top of a very high mountain and showed him all the kingdoms of the world and all the wonderful things in them. The devil said, 'If you will bow down and worship me, I will give you all these things.' Jesus said to him, 'Get away from me, Satan! The Scriptures say, "You must worship the Lord your God. Serve only him!"' So the devil left him. Then some angels came to Jesus and helped him.

(Matthew 4:8–11)

what does the Bible say about FOLLOWING GOD?

First up

It's important to remember that, as with all great adventures, our quest as Christians will face some serious opposition. There is a bad guy. And he doesn't want you to reach your destination. In fact, he'll try to lie, kill, destroy and manipulate everything in your path to keep you from accomplishing the great things that you know God had destined you for. Of course, we're talking about Satan – the devil – and you know what? He doesn't even play fair!

The good news, though, is that God has made a way for us to defeat Satan and all of his wicked schemes against us. It is a fight to the finish, and the ultimate battle has already been won in heaven. In this next section, we'll be looking at some of the ways we as Christians can not only be aware of the devil's tactics, but actually defend ourselves and even begin to fight back in Jesus' name. Remember, greater is the One that's in you than the one that's in the world.

When it comes to God's guidance, be sure you know that you're listening to the right voice. Also know your enemy, and learn how to defeat him.

Name: Paul Campbell

Age: 15

Town: Halesowen

Current status: Music, drama and dance student

You're in a band, right?

Yes.

How do you find inspiration for your songs?

Well, I write the lyrics to my songs, and a girl called Jane gives me the chords. Whatever mood I'm in inspires me to write the lyrics.

Does anything ever stand in your way? What gives you writer's block?

Friends. What people would think about it. I want it to sound good, not too corny.

Do you think the devil ever tries to stop you hearing from God?

Yes. Sometimes I'll think something I'm really not supposed to be thinking. Like when I'm doing something I really shouldn't be doing.

PEOPLE CLIP

what does the Bible say about FOLLOWING GOD? 47

BODY SLAM

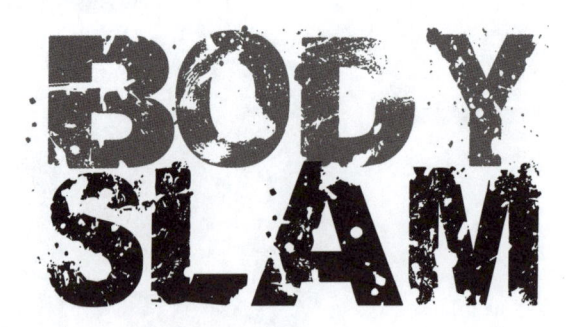

chipK's mind

Don't you just hate it when you think up a great comeback – 5 minutes too late? I'm sure you've experienced this before. Someone says something which really offends you, and you want to say something clever back, but what comes out of your mouth just ends up making you look (and feel) even more stupid than before. Then, once it's too late, you start replaying the scenario over and over in your mind, and *bam*! Something brilliant pops up. You think, 'If only I'd said that instead!'

I remember hearing a guest speaker at my youth group teaching on what Christians call 'spiritual warfare' – the unseen battle between good and evil. Basically, he didn't believe any of it. He said that all this shouting at the devil and binding up demons was just a bunch of baloney, and that all we needed to do as Christians was stand there and eventually the devil would go away. And the worst part is, to my utter shock and horror, the rest of my youth group proceeded to agree with him! I was the only one in the room to openly disagree with the man, but as much as I wanted to publicly win my 'case', at the time I couldn't think of anything clever enough to back it up. It was the perfect example of a humiliating comeback.

Needless to say, I went home and did some serious Word-searching on what spiritual warfare is really all about. My dad helped me to see that we're actually engaged in a full-on WWF wrestling match with the devil from the moment we become Christians. Can you imagine what would happen if you just stood there while the Undertaker danced around the ring and charged at you for one final flying body slam? Not a very pretty picture if you ask me. The Bible clearly says that we need to be aware of Satan's secret war tactics, so that when he fires his missiles of temptation at us, we can fire back with atomic bombs of Scripture, reminding him that Jesus is our master, not him.

God's mind

I did this so that Satan would not win anything from us. We know very well what his plans are.
(2 Corinthians 2:11)

'Since the time John the Baptizer came until now, God's kingdom has been going forward strongly. And people have been trying to take control of it by force.'
(Matthew 11:12)

'But I use the power of God's Spirit to force out demons, and this shows that God's kingdom has already come to you. Whoever wants to enter a strong man's house and steal his things must first tie him up. Then they can steal the things from his house.'
(Matthew 12:28,29)

'They defeated him by the blood sacrifice of the Lamb and by the message of God that they told people. They did not love their lives too much. They were not afraid of death.'
(Revelation 12:11)

When the 72 followers came back from their trip, they were very happy. They said, 'Lord, even the demons obeyed us when we used your name!' Jesus said to them, 'I saw Satan falling like lightning from the sky. He is the enemy, but know that I have given you more power than he has. I have given you power to crush his snakes and scorpions under your feet. Nothing will hurt you. Yes, even the spirits obey you. And you can be happy, but not because you have this power. Be happy because your names are written in heaven.'
(Luke 10:17–20)

'I will give you the keys to God's kingdom. When you speak judgement here on earth, that judgement will be God's judgement. When you promise forgiveness here on earth, that forgiveness will be God's forgiveness.'
(Matthew 16:19)

Our fight is not against people on earth. We are fighting against the rulers and authorities and the powers of this world's darkness. We are fighting against the spiritual powers of evil in the heavenly places.
(Ephesians 6:12)

Your mind

- When was the last time I failed miserably on a great comeback?
- What's my greatest offensive weapon against the devil? (HINT: Ephesians 6:17,18)
- What's the biggest temptation I'm 'wrestling' with at the moment?
- Two practical things I can do to overcome this temptation are:

1.

2.

Chip Kendall, *The Mind Of ChipK: Enter At Your Own Risk*, Authentic, 2005

ReactionReactionReactionReaction

CIRCLE:

TICK:

Total rubbish ☐   Not sure ☐   Worth thinking about ☐   Genius ☐

FILL:

....
....
....
....

Hidden pearls

'I'm pretty certain that in these modern days, one of the ways the devil traps you is through what you watch. There's such rubbish about. There are books now that were banned. You've got to watch what you watch, what you hear, what you read otherwise your mind gets full of rubbish.

If we're watching a programme and it gets bad we turn it off, but when Chip's on TV, we just turn the sound off!'

Fisticuffs

A friend of mine once asked me if I got up every morning prepared to fight, because if I wasn't prepared to fight I might as well stay in bed! Matthew 11:12 says: 'God's kingdom has been going forward strongly. And people have been trying to take control of it by force.' We are in a battle. In Revelation we're told 'it will be terrible for the earth . . . because the devil has gone down to you. He is filled with anger. He knows he doesn't have much time' (Revelation 12:12). In other words, he knows he's going down and boy is he going to make sure he takes as many as he can with him!

Knowing Scripture isn't enough. It isn't for us then to leave it on the bookshelf, pat ourselves on the back, congratulating ourselves that we have read it. We are to use it!

Every time I do something stressful, whether it's sitting an exam, going to a meeting, or going travelling, I have a panicky dream the night before. I dream that I will forget something, or not have thought of something. Exams – what if I forget that I am supposed to bring the book with me? What if there is a section I haven't studied that everybody else knew about? Holidays – what if I turn up at the airport without any money or without my passport? I lie there all night, my mind running through everything I haven't done and all the things that could go wrong and how I could remedy them. I get up in the morning, not only ridiculously stressed, but now also exhausted! I fear being under-prepared all the time.

Ephesians 6 says: 'Depend on the Lord for your strength. Put your trust in his great power. Wear the full armour of God. Wear God's armour so that you can fight against the devil's clever tricks' (Ephesians 6:10,11). The vast majority of the armour is protective – shield, breastplate, helmet. The only weapon as a Christian you are given is the sword of the Spirit – which is the Word of God. **THE BIBLE IS YOUR WEAPON** – with it you are prepared to fight, without it you are lost.

Jesus found Satan. They had an almighty struggle in the desert to see who was going to have the ultimate power. Would Satan fall to Jesus, or would Jesus bow to Satan?

Jesus won. To every temptation Satan threw at him, he always responded with Scripture. Satan could not stand against Scripture, and fled (Luke 4:1–13). There is no argument against Scripture, no room for debate. Satan has no purity in him, and the Bible is the pure Word of God, the two cannot co-exist, therefore one must leave – and it will always be Satan (James 4:7).

> 'The Devil fears the Word of God. He can't bite it; it breaks his teeth' (Martin Luther).

There is a famous quote that states 'the devil's greatest achievement is convincing the world that he doesn't exist'. So often as Christians we forget him, and we need to be reminded that Peter commands us to 'Control yourselves and be careful! The devil, your enemy, goes around like a roaring lion looking for someone to eat' (1 Peter 5:8). The devil does exist, and he doesn't like you – you are his enemy and he is fighting you with everything he's got. But we already have the victory, Jesus defeated him at the cross, and we live in that victory. He is no threat to you if you stand firm. Equip yourself with the knowledge of Scripture. **SATAN IS TERRIFIED OF IT** – because with it you can defeat him. He will therefore try everything to stop you from reading it!

A friend of mine has built herself the full armour of God. She has the helmet, the breastplate, the footwear – everything. Of all the pieces she chooses to give to others to start their own armour collection, she always gives them a sword. You fight from day one, so be prepared!

Andy Frost and Jo Wells, *Freestyle*, **Authentic, 2005**

ReactionReactionReactionReaction

CIRCLE:

😊 ☹️ 😐 😦 😕 😮

TICK:
Total rubbish ☐ Not sure ☐ Worth thinking about ☐ Genius ☐

FILL:

....
....
....
....
....

Spiritual attack

When Christians are at work for God, the devil tries to get in on the act. He is not bothered by Christians who are not a threat to him. In fact, they make his life easy. They do his job for him, making the church seem irrelevant, out of touch, pointless, or constantly fighting with itself.

The devil attacks moving targets, those who threaten his limited power. Have you noticed that when you are trying to be obedient to God, or start praying more, or get involved with some evangelism, life seems to become more difficult? The devil will use illness, problems appearing out of nowhere, disagreements and arguments with people we love, anything he can, to distract you from being the person God wants you to be. God wants us all to be aware of what the devil is capable of, so that we can prepare for attack. But God wants you to remember that if you are a Christian the Holy Spirit lives in you. And he is greater than the devil. (See 1 John 4:4.)

What sort of things does the devil do?

The devil longs to whisper his destructive lies to us. He loves to sow doubt that God is in control of our lives. He tries to make people worship things other than God – even without knowing it. **PRIDE IS ONE OF THE TRAPS** he likes to use. Remember it's the whole reason he fell because he realized that he was a model of perfection and beauty.

The Bible calls the devil the liar, accuser. (Look up John 8:44 and Revelation 12:10,11.) He cannot tell the truth and varies from subtle deception to full-blown lies. We can be free of his power, but we need God's help.

The battleground

People laugh at me because I get scared by the most unscary of films. Even the music in a remotely scary film can have me in bits! But I have learnt that this is God's way of protecting my head and ensuring that my memories and what I dwell on are more pure and innocent. People also think it's odd that I am offended by certain types of TV. Even my Christian friends think it's a bit sweet and eccentric that I can't watch certain things. But I have to go with my own inner conscience and stick to the things I know are important for me. There are some things that disrupt my peace, give me ungodly thoughts or bad dreams. These are the things that I am careful to avoid. – Ems

what does the Bible say about FOLLOWING GOD?

> Brothers and sisters, continue to think about what is good and worthy of praise. Think about what is true and honourable and right and pure and beautiful and respected.

(Philippians 4:8)

If we fill our minds with the sewage of some modern-day films, this will begin to affect our hearts and attitudes. We will start to value the world in a similar way, unless we can filter it out and be aware of it. There may be films, TV programmes, computer games, books or magazines that you are filling your head with that you may need to rethink. Read that verse again from Philippians. Do they measure up to this test? If you are unsure, then the safest thing to do is not to spend time in their company. You have better stuff to fill your head with. Right?

Consequences

When I was at university, some girls came and knocked at my college door. They said that strange things had started happening in their bedroom and they were very scared. They weren't Christians but they knew I was. They asked me to go and pray in the room. As I went in, I could sense a coldness as if a window was open. But it wasn't. They had described how appliances came on by themselves, even when they weren't plugged in. As I prayed, I didn't feel anything dramatic happen, but just a sense that God was now the biggest thing in the room. That was the end of their problems there. – Ems

In this situation something spiritual and unseen was happening. But as with all things that are spiritual, bad or good, they have consequences that we can feel and sometimes see.

When we are full of the Holy Spirit, even people who do not know us can sometimes recognize **SOMETHING DIFFERENT ABOUT US**. There is something special about being filled with 'Godness' that makes a physical difference to us.

We recently heard a story about a famous Christian pop singer whose gig attracted other young artists from the pop world. When asked why they were at the gig, they said, 'We love hanging out with this guy! The rest of the music industry is so dark, but he is just the opposite.'

These young pop stars weren't saying, 'This guy is just bursting with the love of the Lord.' They couldn't have known that, but they could see that there was a lightness about him that was attracting them to him.

So what do people meet when they meet you? Do they see someone full of light, or do they see someone tinged with darkness? There are people who are obviously full of bitterness and pain. Their faces and the way they speak and move show that they are hurt and damaged in some way. Maybe you feel a bit like this and the reason you feel it is because you have been doing things that are not healthy for your mind and body.

What or who is your God?

So what if you have dabbled in things of darkness? What should you do? The Bible is clear that **REPENTANCE IS THE FIRST STEP** whenever we offend God – that's the first thing we should do. We need to put right what is wrong and put behind us all deeds of darkness. It's nearly always really helpful to talk and pray through all of these things with someone mature that we trust. If you have been affected by anything that you have read about here and want to learn how to leave it behind for good, please do something about it.

Ems Hancock and Ian Henderson, *Sorted?*, **Authentic, 2004**

ReactionReactionReactionReaction

CIRCLE:

TICK:

Total rubbish ☐   Not sure ☐   Worth thinking about ☐   Genius ☐

FILL:

Schizophrenic skin

chipK's mind

You've been sentenced to live in an empty padded cell. The straitjacket you're wearing keeps your arms strapped to your body so you can't move them. The only light in your room comes from a single flickering bulb, and just like that bulb, you're all alone.

Or so you think.

No one enters your cell, but a voice enters your head. Then another one joins in. And another. These voices in your head continue to grow louder and louder until your only option is to lose yourself . . . and become one of them.

[cue evil laughter]

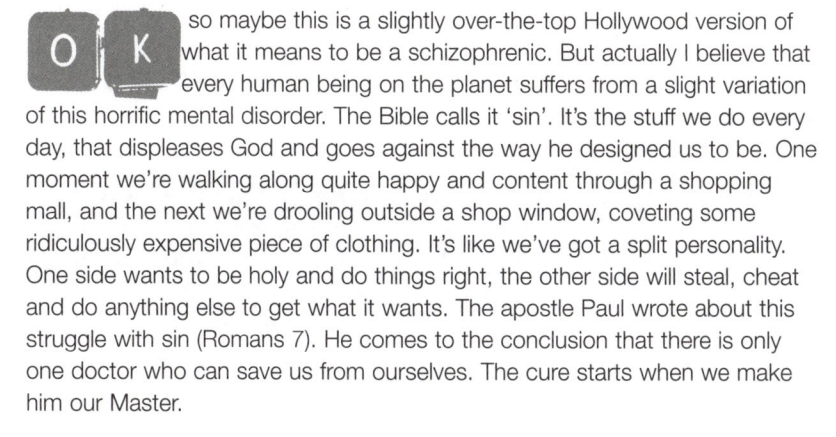

OK so maybe this is a slightly over-the-top Hollywood version of what it means to be a schizophrenic. But actually I believe that every human being on the planet suffers from a slight variation of this horrific mental disorder. The Bible calls it 'sin'. It's the stuff we do every day, that displeases God and goes against the way he designed us to be. One moment we're walking along quite happy and content through a shopping mall, and the next we're drooling outside a shop window, coveting some ridiculously expensive piece of clothing. It's like we've got a split personality. One side wants to be holy and do things right, the other side will steal, cheat and do anything else to get what it wants. The apostle Paul wrote about this struggle with sin (Romans 7). He comes to the conclusion that there is only one doctor who can save us from ourselves. The cure starts when we make him our Master.

I think you know who I'm talking about.

God's mind

We know that the law is spiritual, but I am not. I am so human. Sin rules me as if I were its slave. I don't understand why I act the way I do. I don't do the good I want to do, and I do the evil I hate. And if I don't want to do what I do, that means I agree that the law is good. But I am not really the one doing the evil. It is sin living in me that does it. Yes, I know that nothing good lives in me – I mean nothing good lives in the part of me that is not spiritual. I want to do what is good, but I don't do it. I don't do the good that I want to do. I do the evil that I don't want to do. So if I do what I don't want to do, then I am not really the one doing it. It is the sin living in me that does it. So I have learned this rule: When I want to do good, evil is there with me. In my mind I am happy with God's law. But I see another law working in my body. That law makes war against the law that my mind accepts. That other law working in my body is the law of sin, and that law makes me its prisoner. What a miserable person I am! Who will save me from this body that brings me death? I thank God for his salvation through Jesus Christ our Lord!
(Romans 7:14–25a)

All have sinned and are not good enough to share God's divine greatness. They are made right with God by his grace. This is a free gift. They are made right with God by being made free from sin through Jesus Christ.
(Romans 3:23,24)

Christ had no sin, but God made him become sin so that in Christ we could be right with God.
(2 Corinthians 5:21)

So I tell you, live the way the Spirit leads you. Then you will not do the evil things your sinful self wants. The sinful self wants what is against the Spirit, and the Spirit wants what is against the sinful self. They are always fighting against each other, so that you don't do what you really want to do.
(Galatians 5:16,17)

Those who belong to Christ Jesus have crucified their sinful self. They have given up their old selfish feelings and the evil things they wanted to do.
(Galatians 5:24)

Your mind

- What sins do I struggle with the most? (Hint: be honest!)
- Why are these sins bad? How are they contrary to God's perfect plan, and what are the consequences of doing them?
- Why is Jesus the only person who can start to cure me of my schizophrenic skin? What has to be done that's so important?
- When will I be fully cured?

Chip Kendall, *The Mind Of ChipK: Enter At Your Own Risk*, Authentic, 2005

ReactionReactionReactionReaction

CIRCLE:

TICK: Total rubbish ☐ Not sure ☐ Worth thinking about ☐ Genius ☐

FILL:
....
....
....
....
....

Life lessons

LIFE LESSON THREE

Discipleship and accountability

Follow my example, just as I follow the example of Christ. I praise you because you remember me in all things. You follow closely the teachings I gave you.

(1 Corinthians 11:1,2)

what does the Bible say about FOLLOWING GOD?

First up

In the kingdom of God, there really shouldn't be any 'lone rangers'. Even from the beginning, God said that it wasn't good for man to be alone. Then, after creating the woman for the man, he went on to command them to multiply! Even two just weren't enough. His plan all along has been for us to cultivate relationships with one another as the complete body of Christ.

Jesus taught us to love each other and prayed that all of us would be united as one just like he and the Father are one. Think about that for a second. God himself exists in a relationship. The Father, the Son and the Holy Spirit are our perfect example of unity. The Father sent the Son, the Son sent the Spirit, and the Spirit brings us to complete unity with each other and with God.

And this isn't a shallow unity. Sometimes we humans need to practise tough love and forgive each other even when we don't feel like it. Sometimes we need to confront each other when we're offended. That can be difficult! Especially when we'd much rather just ignore them and do our own thing instead. But when we can still learn to get along, despite our differences – that's when God himself can't help but give his blessing.

LIVING TOGETHER IN PEACE

Oh, how wonderful, how pleasing it is
when God's people all come together as one!
It is like the sweet-smelling oil that is
poured over the high priest's head,
that runs down his beard flowing over his robes.
It is like a gentle rain from Mount Hermon
falling on Mount Zion.
It is there that the LORD has promised
his blessing of eternal life.

(Psalm 133)

So why is all this important when we're talking about following God and his guidance? Because a lot of the time, God chooses to guide us through the godly people around us. He uses them to instruct us, encourage us and even challenge us when we're out of line. This is the essence of discipleship and accountability.

What is discipleship?

Chip talks

If you ask a group of people, 'Who here likes football?' chances are that a lot of them will respond. But within that group, there will almost definitely be varying degrees of football fans. Some of them may enjoy watching a game or two from time to time on television, without necessarily supporting any one particular team. Some may be a little bit more fanatical, with posters on their walls of their favourite player and season tickets to every single match their team plays that year. But then there may be some who absolutely love football. They eat, drink, sleep, poop and pee football. They're passionate about playing it, watching it, wearing it, learning it, talking about it . . . you name it. And they're the ones with their faces painted, singing at the top of their lungs at the front of the crowd in the stadium. Can you think of somebody like that?

The same might be said of some Christians. They're not content with just attending church on a Sunday morning and ticking 'Christian – Other' on their myspace profile. That just wouldn't cut it. They want nothing less than sucking the juice out of every word Jesus ever spoke. They talk about their faith in God openly, and they're not ashamed to practise what they preach. They study the Bible and even memorize it, so that they've always got an answer when people ask them about what they believe and why they believe it. And whenever a question comes up that they can't answer, they simply take it to someone a little wiser to get their perspective, but they certainly don't give up. They're Jesus freaks, through and through. And this is the kind of person that I would call . . . a disciple.

Being a true disciple means that you always persevere, even when the going gets tough. **THE HARD TIMES ONLY SERVE TO MAKE YOU STRONGER.** Someone who's simply 'converted' to Christianity in order to merely 'give it a go' may just as easily decide to convert to another religion to give that one a try. But a disciple, on the other hand, is in for the long haul – for life. A disciple recognizes that his or her life is a journey of discovery, and even though temptation may be lurking just around the corner, they are well equipped with enough spiritual ammo to overcome the devil and press on regardless. Mistakes will be made, but by the grace of God, the disciple's race will be won.

If you're reading this and you're thinking, 'Whoa, that's what I want to be – a disciple,' then take this advice: if you haven't got one already, find a mentor. They don't have to look like Yoda from *Star Wars* or speak like Morpheus from *The Matrix*. It may be one of your parents or your pastor or somebody else from church. Just find somebody who is a little older and wiser than you – someone who's been a Christian for a while longer than you have. Ask them if they would pray about it and consider being your spiritual coach. Give them permission to ask you tough questions and offer sound advice. And then, listen to them. Think about what they say and follow their example as they follow the example of Christ.

Discipleship is something all Christians must undertake in order to fulfil the Great Commission spoken of by Jesus. After all, he said to go and make disciples, not converts. True disciples make disciples. That means nurturing new believers in their faith, helping them to know God better. So let's start doing it!

ReactionReactionReactionReaction

CIRCLE:

☺   ☹   😐   ⁉   😕   😮

TICK:

Total rubbish ☐   Not sure ☐   Worth thinking about ☐   Genius ☐

FILL:

....
....
....
....
....

WHAT IS ACCOUNTABILITY?

Helen talks

Do you have an accountability partner? Being accountable means that you have someone who is going to hold you to account, which is an old fashioned way of saying someone who will check up on you. When you are at school you are accountable to your teacher. She will check up on whether you did your homework or not and will deal with you if you didn't. Once you have a job, you are accountable to your boss, they will check up on whether you are doing your work properly. If they are any good, they will also check if you are happy in your job, if you have the correct skills, or need to learn new ones, and how you are developing as a person. Accountability is really important.

As you grow up, you are expected to be accountable to yourself more and more. The boss who checked up on you every day will check up on you less and less as you become more experienced in your job. In time you may even be the boss and then you might have to take responsibility for yourself and doing your work right without anyone checking up on you. Think about when you were a toddler, your parents checked up on everything, from what you ate to when your nappy needed changing. Imagine if your mum tried checking your pants now! I'm sure you wouldn't be pleased because you don't need to be accountable to anyone else for things like pooping and peeing, eating and sleeping any more. You are able to handle it on your own.

Although growing up means we are able to look after ourselves more, it is still really important to have people in our lives to whom we are accountable. This isn't really something that is encouraged in our society. Society tells us things like, 'you don't need anyone, it's all about looking out for number one', 'older people don't understand young people and can't relate to them', 'no one should tell you what to do' and things like that. **WHAT A LOAD OF RUBBISH**. It is extremely important to have someone in your life who can offer you tough, truthful advice on what to do, and point out when you're in the wrong.

> 'But the gate that opens the way to true life is narrow.
> And the road that leads there is hard to follow.
> Only a few people find it.'
>
> Matthew 7:14

As Christians, we are called to walk a narrow road and the best way to make sure you don't wander off it is to have people in your life who will tell you when you are wandering off it. When you are in the middle of a situation it is not always easy to see when you are going wrong because you are emotionally involved. However, for someone on the outside of the situation, it can be really easy to spot what is happening. For example, you have a fight with your friend. **YOU JUST KNOW THEY ARE WRONG AND YOU ARE RIGHT** and you decide not to speak to them again until they apologize. If you went to an accountability partner and told them about the situation they might be able to see your friend's side of the story, or see that you had a bad attitude, or tell you that you should forgive your friend anyway. They could advise you from an outside, unbiased, objective position.

Equally, having someone you are accountable to can stop you from doing things that you know you shouldn't do. When I was growing up, I had a best friend who was a few years older than me and a really strong Christian. I knew that if I got drunk or did something I shouldn't have, she would ask me about it, and I would have to tell her. Just the thought of that often stopped me doing the wrong thing.

Make sure you choose your accountability partner wisely. They should be truthful, older than you, wiser than you and more mature in their Christian faith. They should be someone you respect and want to please. If you are accountable to someone who you don't care about, knowing they will disapprove of your behaviour is unlikely to stop you misbehaving! They should also be someone you would feel comfortable sharing your problems with and who you know wants the best for you. Having these people in your life will help you grow stronger as a Christian and will help you avoid many of life's pitfalls.

Reaction Reaction Reaction Reaction

CIRCLE:

🙂 🙁 😐 😮 😕 😲

TICK:

Total rubbish ☐   Not sure ☐   Worth thinking about ☐   Genius ☐

FILL:

....
....
....
....

Hidden pearls

'Throughout my life, especially during the war times, I felt that people were praying for me that I would be safe. My friend in the next bed was taken prisoner and I wasn't, I was very happy about that...'

(this happened when Brian was about 20 years old)

GOD'S WILL your desires - THEY FIT

Bible reading Psalm 37:1–7

Enjoy serving the LORD, and he will give you whatever you ask for.
(Psalm 37:4)

'I'm doing all that universal-will stuff,' Natalie says, 'but I have to decide what school to attend and what major to declare and what classes to take. And I have my eye on this guy. Where does he fit into God's plans?'

If you're committed to following God's clear, universal will, it's time to dig in and discover God's specific will day by day. You can seek his plans for you through a four-step process:

1. Seek God's will in the Bible. Knowing Scripture is basic to looking for God's will. If your idea of God's specific will for you doesn't square with Scripture, then it's your will – not God's.

2. Seek God's will in prayer. Jesus taught his disciples to pray, 'Our Father in heaven . . . [may] what you want will be done here on earth, the same as in heaven' (Matthew 6:9,10). God is willing to give you the direction you seek. Ask him for it daily – or as often as you need to!

3. Seek God's will in the counsel of others. God has put wise, mature Christians in your life to help you discern God's specific will. Your parents and other family members, youth leaders, or your pastor might fill that role. Mature believers can speak from a background of experiences you might lack – and their objectivity can keep you from being swayed by your emotions.

4. Seek God's will in your circumstances. God often directs you through outside circumstances beyond your control. If you have musical talents, being offered a scholarship to a top music school might give you a hint that you should pursue a career in music. But keep in mind that circumstances alone don't always clearly indicate God's will. The circumstances you see in your life must be balanced by Scripture, prayer, and the wise counsel of others.

Let's say you're living God's universal will – and you have sought his specific will in Scripture, prayer, counsel, and circumstances. So how do you decide what to do? It's simple. Do what you want to do. If you put God first in your life, he promises to give you the desires of your heart (see Psalm 37:4). And guess what? If what you want somehow doesn't line up with God's will, he will kindly make that clear to you.

REFLECT: WHICH STEPS TO FINDING GOD'S SPECIFIC WILL DO YOU HAVE A HANDLE ON? WHICH DO YOU NEED TO PUT INTO PRACTICE?

PRAY: SPEND A FEW MOMENTS NOW TALKING TO GOD ABOUT HIS WILL IN YOUR LIFE.

Josh McDowell, *Youth Devotions 2*, Tyndale House, 2003

ReactionReactionReactionReaction

CIRCLE:

TICK: Total rubbish ☐   Not sure ☐   Worth thinking about ☐   Genius ☐

FILL:

Prophecy

Don't stop the work of the Holy Spirit. Don't treat prophecy like something that is not important. But test everything. Keep what is good, and stay away from everything that is evil.

(1 Thessalonians 5:19–22)

First up

So far we've looked at loads of different ways we can listen to God's guidance. He speaks to us through prayer, through reading the Bible and through the good advice of other godly people. We've talked about the fact that there is a dark side as well, and an enemy of our souls who wants nothing more than to keep us from hearing God's voice and following his plan for our lives. We've even discussed the importance of discipleship — having a mentor who can regularly speak into your life to encourage and challenge you to be more Christlike. But there's more . . .

All throughout the Bible, we find that God has spoken to his people through prophets. That is, men and women who were filled with the Holy Spirit and able to see into the future as God enabled them. They weren't simply fortune-tellers who merely predicted the future on demand when the price was right. That kind of people have been around for a very long time, and the Bible doesn't have very nice things to say about them! But true prophets really did get their prophecies straight from the heart of God.

When it came to choosing who would be his prophets, God certainly didn't have a particular method or formula. They ranged from being powerful, respectable people like Daniel who was second in command of the entire empire of his day, to being complete social outcasts – crazy people – like Ezekiel, Jeremiah and John the Baptist. There is one thing they all did have in common though. Over time, they were all proven to be true prophets once their prophecies started coming true. For example, check out Isaiah's prophecy about God's suffering servant in the book of Isaiah chapter 53. Surely he was talking about Jesus. But wait a second. This guy wrote this stuff 750 years before Jesus was even born! Pretty convincing proof that he was truly a prophet of God.

72 what does the Bible say about FOLLOWING GOD?

First up

There are some Christians today who believe that true prophets aren't around anymore. They'll tell you that every prophecy that's really from God has already been written about in the Bible. This has not been our experience. Over the course of our lives we've undoubtedly encountered people still being used by God to speak prophetically to us today. They make no attempt to rewrite the Bible or twist something God spoke thousands of years ago. In fact, their prophecies are always in line with what the Bible says. If they weren't, then we would have refused to have anything to do with what they had spoken.

So we want to encourage you to make up your own mind about what you believe. Are prophets and prophecies still around today? Do they really match up to God's ultimate standard for living – the Bible? Are they useful to us when it comes to following God's guidance? We believe so. But judge for yourself.

PROPHECY today?

chipK's mind

In 1999, my dad and I had the amazing privilege of travelling to Kampala, Uganda, to be a part of AfriCamp, an annual conference for around 2,000 Africans. I'll never forget the atmosphere in that giant tent, as so many believers came together to worship God and receive amazing teaching from some of the world's most prophetic voices.

One of the speakers that year was Cindy Jacobs, a woman of God who is famous for prophesying over people (telling them what she believes God is saying about them, by describing what will happen in the future). It wasn't the first time anyone had prophesied over me, but this was certainly the most *specific* prophecy I'd ever been given. She talked about my future wife, my education, and my gifting as a speaker. She went on to say, 'I see a room full of instruments . . . what name am I getting? A Roland . . . God is going to put together a band of youth that will go all over the world.' Well, to cut a long story short, 3 years later I was married to Helen (who I'd met at Bible College in the USA) and preaching the gospel all over the world as a part of thebandwithnoname. And to top it all off, Zarc Porter (our producer) used Roland equipment almost exclusively in the early days of the band. How accurate was that?!

I fully believe that prophecy is not just something God relegated to Bible times, but something he is still using today. However, it's important that we remember a few biblical guidelines when it comes to handling prophetic words.

Always use discernment. There is such a thing as a false prophet. They were around in Bible times and they're certainly around nowadays. 'Discernment' means distinguishing between what comes from God and what doesn't. Be sure to weigh up a prophetic word with Scripture, and try to make sure the person giving you the prophecy is sound.

Take as confirmation, not direction. What I mean is this: if someone says God is going to give you a lot of children, and you're not even married yet, it's probably not the wisest thing in the world to just go and marry the first person you find who wants lots of kids. Don't try to make a prophecy come to pass. Wait for God's timing.

Run it by your pastor. It's always a good idea to seek the counsel of a mentor or someone who is more spiritually mature than you are. That way you know you're covered.

God's mind

Love should be the goal of your life, but you should also want to have the gifts that come from the Spirit. And the gift you should want most is to be able to prophesy. I will explain why. Those who have the gift of speaking in a different language are not speaking to people. They are speaking to God. No one understands them – they are speaking secret things through the Spirit. But those who prophesy are speaking to people. They help people grow stronger in faith, and they give encouragement and comfort. Those who speak in a different language are helping only themselves. But those who prophesy are helping the whole church. I would like all of you to have the gift of speaking in different languages. But what I want more is for you to prophesy. Anyone who prophesies is more important than those who can only speak in different languages. However, if they can also interpret those languages, they are as important as the one who prophesies. If they can interpret, then the church can be helped by what they say.
(1 Corinthians 14:1–5)

'I will pour out my Spirit on all kinds of people. Your sons and daughters will prophesy, your old men will have special dreams, and your young men will see visions.'
(Joel 2:28)

We all have different gifts. Each gift came because of the grace God gave us. Whoever has the gift of prophecy should use that gift in a way that fits the kind of faith they have.
(Romans 12:6)

Solid food is for people who have grown up. From their experience they have learned to see the difference between good and evil.
(Hebrews 5:14)

The Spirit gives to one person the power to do miracles, to another the ability to prophesy.
(1 Corinthians 12:10a)

Your mind

- **What has been prophesied over me?**
- **Do I have the gift of prophecy?** ☐ Yes ☐ No
- **When have I ever used the gift of prophecy?**
- **Here is my prayer: that God would begin/continue to use me in a prophetic way.**

Reaction Reaction Reaction Reaction

CIRCLE:

☺ ☹ 😐 😦 🙁 😲

TICK:

Total rubbish ☐   Not sure ☐   Worth thinking about ☐   Genius ☐

FILL:

....
....
....

Name: **David**
Age: **21**
Town: **Beer Sheva, Israel**
Current Status: **soldier in the IDF**

What cologne do you use?

Georgio Armani

What is God doing among your friends in the army?

Everyone has just gone through a war, so it's been very heart-softening. No one has any hope, so they're all willing to listen to anyone with hope and people with answers to thousands of years of persecution.

How would you define prophecy?

God's impartation of information regarding the future or insight into people's lives.

PEOPLE CLIP

76 what does the Bible say about FOLLOWING GOD?

MOVING IN THE PROPHETIC

God might show you a picture or suggest a Bible verse to read. He might give you a sense of something, a feeling, a word or sentence. He might speak to you in a conversation or through a dream. What about asking God to speak through a film or the book you're reading? Looking at a piece of art? Like with Elijah, we need to be expectant that God will speak, but open as to how he will do it.

I was travelling home on the train one day, minding my own business, when I spotted out of the corner of my eye a lady slumped over on her seat crying quietly to herself, oblivious to those around her. As I watched her, I asked God why she was so upset. I asked God to tell me what had happened to her that had made her so utterly miserable?

In my mind I heard **'SING O BARREN WOMAN'**. Yeah right that was God! What a cliché! You see a woman in her twenties and you automatically think 'man trouble' or 'kids'.

'That's not God that's just me', I thought to myself. But the voice continued 'You who never bore a child . . . your descendants will cover the earth' (from Isaiah 54). 'Come on God,' I thought to myself, 'give me something I can work with here.' I didn't dare share those words with her – I could have been completely wrong and then what would she have thought?! I could have ended up looking really stupid.

But I couldn't ignore the prompting and as we both stood up to get off the train, I asked her if she was alright. 'Tell her what I've said,' I heard God say. 'No,' I replied, 'let's see what she says first.'

She looked up at me through her thick eye make-up and matted hair, and sighed. 'He dumped me,' she said. 'I can't have kids and he dumped me.'

I COULDN'T BELIEVE IT! I had heard God right and missed my opportunity. I walked home kicking myself. God had spoken, I had heard him and yet I had done nothing for fear of embarrassment.

Although we might be happy to go along with the idea that God will speak to us. It's harder to trust when it's God talking to us about other people. When God speaks, it's often easy to ignore him, thinking it's just us, or that we're imagining things. But God has always spoken to people, calling them out of their tiny concept of the world, into a mind-blowing relationship with him. He asks us to be his mouthpieces.

Fear stops us from asking for the gift of prophecy, and fear certainly stops many of us from using it. But God charges us? 'Don't stop the work of the Holy Spirit. Don't treat prophecy like something that is not important. But test everything. Keep what is good, and stay away from everything that is evil' (1 Thessalonians 5:19–22). Therefore if we are worried that we might be speaking our own words despite our best intentions, God doesn't want us to be afraid. 'Try it out,' he says. If you're wrong just discard it. Ask others with discernment and see what is of God and what isn't. If you are right then it will be all good! Paul commands us to eagerly ask God for the gift of prophecy (1 Corinthians 14:1). Let's not pass up on the opportunity to witness God speaking to others through us.

Andy Frost and Jo Wells, *Freestyle***, Authentic, 2005**

ReactionReactionReactionReaction

CIRCLE:

😊 ☹️ 😐 😮 😕 😲

TICK:

Total rubbish ☐   Not sure ☐   Worth thinking about ☐   Genius ☐

FILL:

....
....
....
....
....

Reality Check

MAKING DISCIPLESHIP WORK FOR *ME*

Take some time to carefully consider the following:

When is the best time of the day for me to meet up with a mentor?

- a early morning
- b afternoon
- c evening
- d OTHER: ....

Who do I know that is best suited for this role and available at that time of day?

- a parent
- b teacher
- c pastor
- d youth leader
- e OTHER: ....

How often will I commit to meeting up with my mentor?

- a once a week
- b once every two weeks
- c once a month
- d OTHER: ....

Things I'd like to pray about and discuss with my mentor when we meet:

home life: ....

church life: ....

school / work life: ....

personal struggles: ....

OTHER: ....

Right now, I set a deadline for myself of finding a mentor by:

day .... month .... year ....

Signed:

....

Date: ....

**DON'T DELAY!
PICK UP THE PHONE AND CALL NOW!
THE SOONER THE BETTER!**

LIFE LESSON FOUR

'Follow me'

So he came to them and said, 'All authority in heaven and on earth is given to me. So go and make followers of all people in the world. Baptize them in the name of the Father and the Son and the Holy Spirit. Teach them to obey everything that I have told you to do. You can be sure that I will be with you always. I will continue with you until the end of time.'

(Matthew 28:18–20)

what does the Bible say about FOLLOWING GOD?

First up

The beautiful thing about being followers of Christ is that even though each of us will be guided down different paths, we all have the same mission. When Jesus gave us the 'Great Commission' to make disciples of every nation, he wasn't only speaking to his handful of followers at the time. He understood that even now, 2,000 years later, all the millions of Christians all around the world must be unified if we're ever going to accomplish what each of us has been called to individually. He was speaking to us. Our purpose is to know Jesus and to make him known.

We've made this the theme of our final lesson in this book on following God and his guidance simply because sharing your faith is without a doubt the most significant thing you'll ever do down here on earth. There are many things we'll get to do in heaven, like worship God extravagantly, have huge parties around God's throne, meet up with old friends we haven't seen for ages and get some top rate Bible teaching from the prophets and teachers who wrote it all down in the first place! But the one exciting thing we won't be able to do in heaven is witness to people about Jesus. By then it'll be too late. The ones who are destined for heaven will already be there, and the ones who weren't given the opportunity to respond to Christ will not be there. It is up to us to shine the light we've been given. People's souls hang in the balance. The apostle Paul wrote these words:

> But before people can pray to the Lord for help, they must believe in him. And before they can believe in the Lord, they must hear about him. And for anyone to hear about the Lord, someone must tell them. And before anyone can go and tell them, they must be sent. As the Scriptures say, 'How wonderful it is to see someone coming to tell good news!'

(Romans 10:14,15)

The Good News is so good that it deserves to be told everywhere. Will you tell it? Will you dedicate the rest of your life to telling it? Will you show tough love by telling it to the people closest to you who don't yet know God, and even telling it to the ones who would consider themselves enemies of God? The command has been given but the choice is yours.

One thing is for certain. When it comes to sharing your faith in Jesus, you cannot use the excuse, 'Well, I just couldn't get any guidance . . .'

WHOSE RULES WILL RULE?

Bible reading: Deuteronomy 10:12–16

> The LORD your God wants you to respect him and do what he says ... So obey the laws and commands of the LORD that I am giving you today. These laws and commands are for your own good.

(Deuteronomy 10:12,13)

'You know,' Carmen insists, **'I want to do what's right. But I hear so many things from so many people that I don't know what's right any more. I'm like a little kid playing baseball. I've got coaches and team mates and my parents and the other team all yelling at me at once. I need to know what God wants.'**

Confused as Carmen is, she's taken a huge step toward obeying God: she wants what God wants. Truth is, the struggle isn't figuring out right and wrong. It's deciding God's version of right and wrong is better than your own or anything anyone else yells at you. Once you have decided to follow God's absolute best, here's a step by step plan to figure out what he wants:

1. Consider the choice. Through Jesus Christ and the words of Scripture, God has revealed his absolute standards for right and wrong. You have many big choices to make in life, but the biggest is deciding whose version of right and wrong you will live by.

2. Compare it to God. Your next step is to compare an attitude or action to who God is and what he has said about it.

3. Commit to God's way. God has promised that when you submit to him as Saviour and Lord of your life, he will pump you full of his power to live according to his ways. Here's how to get filled:

    a. Turn from your selfish ways and confess your sin (see 1 John 1:9). Sincerely turn your back on sin and claim God's free forgiveness.

    b. Turn control of you life over to the Lord. If God can keep planets spinning, rivers running, and seasons coming and going, don't you think he can keep your life in order if you give him control?

c. Trust God to fill you and lead you by his Holy Spirit. Being filled with the Holy Spirit means he directs your life and gives you his power to resist temptation, gain courage, make right choices, and deal with whatever happens to you.

d. Keep walking in the power of the Spirit. As you live in the power of the Holy Spirit, you can live more consistently day after day.

4. Count on God's protection and provision. Living according to God's way brings countless spiritual blessings like freedom from guilt, a clear conscience, the joy of sharing Christ, and most importantly, the love and smile of God.

REFLECT: ARE YOU SEEKING GOD'S VERSION OF RIGHT AND WRONG FOR YOUR LIFE? HOW DO YOU SEE THAT HAPPENING IN YOUR DAILY DECISIONS?

PRAY: ASK FOR HELP TO APPLY GOD'S STANDARDS TO YOUR ATTITUDES AND ACTIONS.

Josh McDowell, *Youth Devotions 2*, **Tyndale House, 2003**

ReactionReactionReactionReaction

CIRCLE:

☺ ☹ 😐 ⁉ 🙁 😮

TICK:

Total rubbish ☐   Not sure ☐   Worth thinking about ☐   Genius ☐

FILL:

....
....
....
....

EPIC TALES

I love hearing those stories about 'old school' missionaries who preach in faraway countries that you only ever read about in geography lessons. You hear their tales of meeting tribes with pointy spears and war paint, and about how they led entire civilizations to Christ. Then you hear about those stories of evangelists in urban settings that get attacked and beaten up by gun-wielding gangsters. They, too, share stories of seeing entire gangs transformed as they enter into a relationship with God. Maybe these are the kind of images that you think of when you hear the word 'evangelist'. Or perhaps you conjure up a picture of a smartly-dressed preacher, in a shirt and tie, preaching on a big stage. A Billy Graham-type figure in a stadium stacked with people.

All of these examples of evangelists are great. But when I was growing up, I often felt totally insignificant in comparison. I wanted exciting stories to share like they had but I often doubted if I could really be an evangelist. **WHO WAS I TO SHARE JESUS WITH PEOPLE?** Day by day, I would list excuses rather than giving it a go. I decided that when I knew the Bible well enough, when I could discern the voice of God fully and when I had undergone lots of training on mission, then I would be ready. But at present I just wasn't qualified.

Even the book of Acts scared me as I read mega-cool stories of Paul's mission trips that were stacked with adventure and tough times – Paul was shipwrecked, stoned by an angry mob and flogged for the gospel. Pretty full-on! But we need to remember that the word 'evangelist' simply means 'a messenger of good news'. We must hold these stories in perspective – though we are all called to share Jesus, this doesn't mean that we all have to move to Africa or book our local football stadium. God wants to use us, our relationships and our gifts to share our faith. Once we have entered a relationship with Jesus, we are called to 'go' and tell others.

'GO!'
But why don't we want to?

In Matthew, Mark, Luke and Acts, Jesus is recorded as giving the 'Great Commission' to the disciples. This commission is the last instruction to go and tell others about him. This is the last thing that Jesus is recorded as saying before he ascends into heaven, and this shows something of its importance. He did not tell us to build church buildings but to make disciples. This Great Commission is as relevant today as it was for the disciples 2,000 years ago. He has left the most amazing message in history in our hearts, and we, as the church, are called to go and share it.

The Great Commission is pretty clear on the whole issue of evangelism. We are told to 'go'. There is not much room for discussion here – Jesus doesn't ask, **'DO YOU FANCY A BIT OF MISSION, CHAPS?'** He tells us to 'Go!' This indicates something of the importance and urgency of the task we have been given. But as with all aspects of discipleship, this is not some chore that we should feel obligated to do. Evangelism, being involved in God's plan to save the world, should be a joy and a privilege. It's pretty awesome that he allows us to be a part of this process.

So it is not merely because we are commanded to make disciples that we do evangelism or that we want to score Brownie points with God. We have this life-transforming message in our hearts – what else are we going to do with it? We should *want* to go. We should *want* people to have meaning and purpose in their lives. We should *want* others to have their sin forgiven. We should *want* others to receive the gift of eternal life. This is such an important message we need other people to hear it. Jesus said, 'The only way to the Father is through me' (John 14:6).

Andy Frost and Jo Wells, *Freestyle***, Authentic, 2005**

ReactionReactionReactionReaction

CIRCLE:

☺ ☹ 😐 ⚠ 😕 😨

TICK:

Total rubbish ☐   Not sure ☐   Worth thinking about ☐   Genius ☐

FILL:

....
....
....
....

Hidden pearls

'You've just got to throw caution to the wind and tell your friends that you love Jesus and that he's always with you. If your friends don't like it they can lump it!'

what does the Bible say about FOLLOWING GOD? 87

COMMISSIONED 110 PER CENT

Bible reading: 1 Corinthians 9:16

> It's not my work of telling the Good News that gives me any reason to boast. That is my duty – something I must do. If I don't tell people the Good News, I am in real trouble.

(1 Corinthians 9:16)

Jasmine didn't like Mission Fest, an annual conference at her church reminding the congregation of its assignment to reach the world. Every year one or two speakers always made her feel like spiritual slime. They were the ones who had a table at the back of the room for sign-ups to go to Timbuktu – today.

You might wonder what it really means to commit yourself for life to fulfilling the Great Commission as a rescuer and discipler of non-Christians. It doesn't mean God drags you screaming to the other side of the world. It simply means:

- You always have a list of non-Christians you are praying for – family members, friends, classmates, neighbours, people you work with, etc.
- You are always making time to relate to and build bridges of communication with the non-Christians God is calling you to reach.
- You are always prepared to share a clear presentation of the gospel.
- You are always ready to disciple those who trust Christ.

If you're tempted to think that being a rescuer is a chore, remember several things:

- You are privileged to join with God in his mission to liberate people living in darkness. Sharing him with others is one way you worship him and thank him for rescuing you.

- You are empowered for what you are called to do. The Holy Spirit within you makes you totally adequate for the task.
- You will prevail. As you let the Holy Spirit lead and empower you, you will see non-Christians rescued from the dominion of darkness and transferred into the kingdom of God.

Being a lifetime rescuer and discipler isn't a job, it's a lifestyle. So whether you're at school, at work, in a restaurant, at a game, at a party, or whatever, you're on duty. And you don't get to retire. God has two ways to let you know when to stop? RIP or rapture. Until then, you're still on active duty as a rescuer.

REFLECT: SAY IT IN YOUR OWN WORDS: WHAT DOES IT MEAN FOR YOU TO BE A DISCIPLER FOR LIFE?

PRAY: ASK GOD TO GUIDE YOU IN THE MINISTRY OF DISCIPLING THAT BEST FITS THE GIFTS HE HAS GIVEN YOU.

Josh McDowell, *Youth Devotions 2*, Tyndale House, 2003

ReactionReactionReactionReaction

CIRCLE:

TICK:

Total rubbish ☐   Not sure ☐   Worth thinking about ☐   Genius ☐

FILL:

Hidden pearls

'We often find it's easier if you talk about something that's happened. Ask, "Don't you think there's a reason why this happened?" You can let them know where you stand as a Christian.'

Practical help

Never stop praying. Be ready for anything by praying and being thankful. Also pray for us. Pray that God will give us an opportunity to tell people his message. I am in prison for doing this. But pray that we can continue to tell people the secret truth that God has made known about Christ. Pray that I will say what is necessary to make this truth clear to everyone.

(Colossians 4:2–4)

First up

Wow, you've almost reached the end of the book! Well done. By now we've hopefully given you a good overall picture of what the Bible says about following God and receiving his guidance. You've learned how to hear and recognise God's voice. You've read about overcoming the obstacles Satan throws in your way. You've understood how important it is to get some quality discipleship and you've even got a better idea of what the Great Commission is all about. But the question still remains: so now what?

We thought it would be a good idea to finish with some simple, quality advice. A little bit of practical help to show you what it actually looks like to follow God and trust him for guidance. These are things that we would encourage you to pray about making a part of your daily routine – things like praying, reading and memorizing the Bible, and reaching out to the people around you with the love of Jesus.

The plans and destiny that God has for you are completely unique to you. Treasure them deep inside your heart. Write them down as God reveals them to you. You might need to remind yourself of them later! The ways in which God reveals himself to you may be different than the methods he uses with other Christians around you. The important thing is that you always trust in him to guide you.

Don't just settle for following the patterns of this world. Stuff like going out and getting wasted with your friends, or using people to give yourself a boost up the career ladder, or making as much money as you can so you can have the next big thing. It's the 'normal' people who freak out over finding the right university and landing the biggest paying job. Instead, we should be like King David who wrote: 'Some give the credit for victory to their chariots and soldiers, but we honour the LORD our God' *(Psalm 20:7)*.

First up

There have been many times in our own lives when we've been tempted to follow our own understanding instead of trusting in God's seemingly ridiculous guidance. But over and over, God has always come through on his promises and proven that his way is better than ours. We've trusted in him and he has cleared the road for us to follow. We're not lying or making this stuff up! Our own experience has led us to wholeheartedly endorse to you what the Bible says about following God and his guidance.

The following is our prayer for you as you continue to follow God and seek his guidance:

Father, thank you for being so trustworthy. Please give guidance and direction to whoever is reading this right now. Teach them to hear your voice and obey it. Clear away all the distractions and confirm what you are saying to them. Help them to devote themselves to putting this good advice into action. Give them your Spirit to comfort, challenge and empower them to do your will. We pray that they wouldn't settle for a mediocre existence, but they would always explore the new faith journeys you lead them on with the heart of an adventurer. And most of all, show them how much you truly love them. In Jesus' Name, amen.

BUT HOW?

So you are up for sharing Jesus with people? But then comes the question – how on earth do we actually do it? The 'evangelism' word seems so scary! It is in fact not as hard as we often think and we are often doing it in many ways already. Every day there are opportunities to share Jesus. We just need to start looking for them. I find one of the easiest ways to understand evangelism is in the concept of sowing and reaping.

We live in a society where we want everything fast. Rather than working hard to earn money, people buy a lottery ticket – thinking 'it could be me'. Rather than 'cheffing' up a classic pasta dish, we head down to McDonald's. Rather than dieting and exercising to lose weight, why not get liposuction (nice). I even get those emails that tell me 'Why study hard when you can buy a degree on-line?' Bargain.

I believe that in our culture, where we want immediate results and are often unwilling to put in the hard graft, if things don't happen quickly we often can't be bothered at all. Some Christians have adopted this attitude when it comes to their faith. They want fast converts and if there is not an immediate response they give up or move on.

As I read the Bible, I am amazed how much it talks about sowing for a harvest. Though God sometimes does the miraculous, perhaps we as Christians don't always want to sow. **I BELIEVE OUR PROBLEM IS THAT WE JUST DON'T GET THE WHOLE SOWING CONCEPT**. The nearest most of us come to farming today is growing cress on cotton wool in primary school. Yet in Bible times, they had to work the land, turn the solid earth and endure the seasons. They were dependent on good crops and couldn't just pop down to ASDA for a pre-packaged salad or microwave lasagne.

The Bible calls us to sow in abundance: 'The one who plants few seeds will have a small harvest. But the one who plants a lot will have a big harvest' (2 Corinthians 9:6). I want to abundantly sow Jesus into our schools, our colleges, our workplaces and our homes. We need to sow love and truth where the world has sown hate and lies.

Pornography has devalued sex, media coverage of events has increased our fear, and magazines dictate our self-esteem and image. What has been sown is now being reaped. Yet we can see the tides change. We can see a different harvest. All we need to do is start sowing love. Though we may feel that we have so little to give, we can all sow love. We do not have to be great communicators or greatly experienced mission experts. Jesus spoke about the faith of a mustard seed being enough to move mountains. With the love that we can share, we can go the extra mile, the love that calls us to care for the marginalized and the poor, the love that is more than lip-service, the love that knows no limits.

Andy Frost and Jo Wells, *Freestyle*, Authentic, 2005

ReactionReactionReactionReaction

CIRCLE:

TICK: Total rubbish ☐ Not sure ☐ Worth thinking about ☐ Genius ☐

FILL:

Name: Helen Sare

Age: 19½ years old

Town: Cambridgeshire

Current status: Intern as Urban Community Worker with Baptist Union, Bristol

Fave colour: green

How often do you read the Bible?

Every morning while eating breakfast. It's the best way to start the day.

How has God spoken to you?

The other day I was praying with some youth leaders. We were praying about a guy named Johnny who wasn't a Christian but came to Soul Survivor with his friends. I got this word in my head while we were praying. 'Hammock'. Weird word, I know. So I said it out loud and asked if it meant anything to the people there. The youth leader looked at me like, what are you on about. Then he remembered that Johnny had said if he came back to SS, he would bring his hammock.

What does that mean?

I'm hoping it means that he'll come back.

Why do you want him to come back?

So he can actually learn to leave his baggage at the cross and have a relationship with God.

GETTING TO KNOW GOD

When it comes to spending time with the big 'G', I can be shocking. My Bible reading and prayer times are sometimes 'not-so-daily'. I try to make up excuses in my own mind, but nothing ever makes up for the fact that it's so easy to put other things before God. I have found myself literally having to make myself sit down and read the Bible, and I bet 99% of Christians have experienced the same feeling! Let's take a look at how we can get the funk-factor back into our quiet times with God.

1. First of all, when you're not feeling in the flow of your quiet times, **DON'T BEAT YOURSELF UP ABOUT IT**. Everyone has been there at least once and I can pretty much guarantee it will happen again and again at different stages in your life. The most important thing is that you get through it and don't give up. But the fact that everyone goes through it is not an excuse to stop trying. You have to keep fighting to get back on track – don't let Satan tempt you into thinking less of yourself just because you haven't read your Bible. God will always love you no matter what.

2. Secondly, **DECIDE TO DO SOMETHING ABOUT IT**. Take a trip to your local Christian bookstore and find a study guide for young people. Maybe the Bible you have at the moment is written in old-fashioned English and you need a Bible that transforms God's Word into something you can understand and relate to. If that's the case, I would recommend the *Youth Bible* or the *Street Bible* – both of them are really good Bibles for young people who want to get stuck into God's Word. I have found that reading

The Word 4U 2Day or other daily devotions is another way of focusing on a particular section of the Bible without feeling that you're doing it on your own. Those kinds of things really help you to understand bits that you may not have understood if you were just reading through the Bible on your own.

3. Thirdly, **PRAY ABOUT IT**. God knows exactly how you're feeling about everything. Ask God to help you get a grip on reading the Bible and praying. Ask him to motivate and encourage you when you're finding it boring. Reading the Bible can be really exciting and it's great to get to know more about God. I admit that sometimes it can be really hard work, but stick with it. Don't give up on God and the mind-blowing power of his word in the Bible. It really is life-changing!

Shell Perris, *Something to Shout About,* **Authentic, 2006**

ReactionReactionReactionReaction

CIRCLE:

TICK:

Total rubbish ☐   Not sure ☐   Worth thinking about ☐   Genius ☐

FILL:

....
....
....
....

TIME OUT

Bible reading Mark 6:45–56

He went up into the hills to pray.
(Mark 6:46)

Your youth pastor might rant. Your parents may hand you a Bible and this devotional book! You might even have been hit with, 'If Jesus needed to spend time alone with his Father, how much more do you need to spend time with God?'

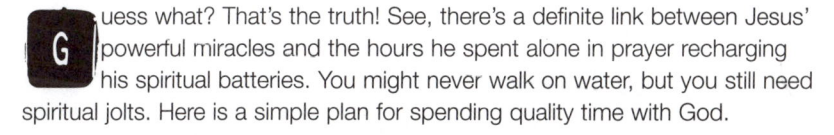

Guess what? That's the truth! See, there's a definite link between Jesus' powerful miracles and the hours he spent alone in prayer recharging his spiritual batteries. You might never walk on water, but you still need spiritual jolts. Here is a simple plan for spending quality time with God.

1. **Get alone with God**. Our noisy, pushy, in-your-face culture doesn't make it easy to find a place to be alone with God. But if you think hard enough, you can discover a place where no one will disturb you. If you have a bedroom with privacy, use it to get alone with God. If you share a room with a brother or sister, look for another place – a storage room, attic, garage, or basement. When you get alone with God, get comfortable so you can concentrate. If you're uptight when you sit, lie down and relax. Kneeling might put you in the right frame of mind when you need to talk to God about something serious.

2. **Talk to God**. Just talk to him as if he were sitting alongside you. Tell him about your anger, frustration, happiness, thankfulness, anything, everything. You can even say, 'Lord, I don't feel like talking to you today, but I will because I know it's good for me.' How you talk isn't as important as how honest you are. If talking to God bores you, it's time to find a different way to communicate with him. You can write God a letter, sing him a song, or read Scripture to him. Use your imagination.

3. Let God talk to you. If you give God the chance, he will talk to you. Not out loud, perhaps, but through the Bible and through your thoughts and ideas. The Bible is the main way God talks to you today. Make a point to tell God that you want to hear what he has to say to you. Then read a few verses during your quiet time and mull over them for a while. Listen to some Christian music, read a solid Christian book or magazine, or just ponder what God has done.

God probably won't ask you to heal crowds like Jesus did. But God has plans for you, and you will be ready for those plans each day after some quiet time with God.

REFLECT: WHAT CHANGES MIGHT GIVE YOU BETTER TIMES ALONE WITH GOD?

PRAY: GOD, USE THE TIMES WE TALK TOGETHER TO GET ME READY FOR THE COOL THINGS YOU HAVE FOR ME TO DO.

Josh McDowell, *Youth Devotions 2*, Tyndale House, 2003

ReactionReactionReactionReaction

CIRCLE:

TICK:
Total rubbish ☐   Not sure ☐   Worth thinking about ☐   Genius ☐

FILL:
....
....
....
....
....

Reality Check

MY PERSONAL STRATEGY

Carefully consider which of these you will implement into your daily devotions/worship routine.

Prayer

I will write lists of the names of the following people and commit to praying for them every day:

- Unsaved friends/relatives
- Family members
- Close friends
- My church community (including my pastor and elders)
- My school/work community (including my teachers/employers)
- My nation (including my government leaders)
- OTHER: _____

Bible reading

I will commit to reading my Bible every day because it is my spiritual food.

- How much will I read per day?
- When will I aim to finish reading the entire Bible?
- 'One Year Bibles' are available online and in bookstores. Will I buy one?
- Which passages will I memorize?

what does the Bible say about FOLLOWING GOD?

Meditation

Not the dodgy kind! Which of these will I begin to put into practice in order to know God better?

- Listening to a worship song on an MP3 player or CD
- Taking a walk to enjoy God's character revealed in his creation
- Lighting candles as a symbolic act
- Waiting silently before God
- Writing in a journal
- Reading quality Christian books with sound advice
- OTHER: _____

Sharing my faith

I am a disciple of Christ commissioned to make more disciples. I will commit to doing the following:

- Speak to my unsaved friends about my faith in Jesus
- Do my best to answer their questions about God, no matter how tough the questions might be
- Invite them to church and other outreach events
- Ask them if they have any specific prayer requests and if they're happy for me to pray for them
- Be a good witness in the way I live my life
- Join a Christian Union at my school or workplace. And if there isn't one, start one!

Further Recommendations

We'd like to encourage you to consider joining one of these online communities, which we believe will help you to manage and monitor your spiritual growth:

www.battlecry.com

www.hope-revolution.com

www.liveaudacious.com

www.ihop.org

www.24-7prayer.com